CONTENTS

H.R. 3137, A BILL TO AMEND THE PRESIDENTIAL TRANSITION ACT OF 1963

WEDNESDAY, OCTOBER 13, 1999

HOUSE OF REPRESENTATIVES,
SUBCOMMITTEE ON GOVERNMENT MANAGEMENT,
INFORMATION, AND TECHNOLOGY,
COMMITTEE ON GOVERNMENT REFORM,
Washington, DC.

The subcommittee met, pursuant to notice, at 10 a.m., in room 2154, Rayburn House Office Building, Hon. Stephen Horn (chairman of the subcommittee) presiding.

Present: Representatives Horn, Ose, and Turner.

Staff present: Russell George, staff director/ chief counsel; Matthew Ebert, policy advisor; Bonnie Heald, director of communications/professional staff member; Chip Ahlswede, clerk; P.J. Caceres and Deborah Oppenheim, interns; Trey Henderson, minority counsel; and Jean Gosa, minority staff assistant.

Mr. HORN. A quorum being present, this hearing of the Subcommittee on Government Management, Information, and Technology will come to order.

Until 1963, the primary source of funding for Presidential transitions was the incoming President's political party and the contributions of volunteer staff. The Presidential Transition Act of 1963 was enacted to authorize Federal funding and assistance for incoming Presidents. It also provided the authority for the outgoing President and Vice President to use the funds for their transition into private life for up to 6 months. The act authorized the appropriation of $900,000 to be divided equally between the incoming and outgoing administrations.

In 1976, Congress amended the Presidential Transition Act of 1963 to increase the funding provided in the 1963 act.

In 1988, Congress passed the Presidential Transition Effectiveness Act, which again raised the funding for Presidential transitions, and included a provision that calls for annual adjustments for inflation. In addition, the 1988 act required that all preelection transition funds must be acquired privately, and the names of all transition personnel and private contributors are publicly disclosed.

[The information referred to follows:]

PRESIDENTIAL TRANSITION ACT OF 1963
P.L. 88-277; MARCH 7, 1964; 78 STAT.153

Text:

AN ACT

To promote the orderly transfer of the executive power in connection with the expiration of the term of office of a President and the inauguration of a new President.

Be it enacted by the Senate and House of Representatives of the United States of America in Congress assembled, That this Act may be cited as the "Presidential Transition Act of 1963."

PURPOSE OF THIS ACT

SEC. 2. The Congress declares it to be the purpose of this Act to promote the orderly transfer of the executive power in connection with the expiration of the term of office of a President and the inauguration of a new President. The national interest requires that such transitions in the office of President be accomplished so as to assure continuity in the faithful execution of the laws and in the conduct of the affairs of the Federal Government, both domestic and foreign. Any disruption occasioned by the transfer of the executive power could produce results detrimental to the safety and well-being of the United States and its people. Accordingly, it is the intent of the Congress that appropriate actions be authorized and taken to avoid or minimize any disruption. In addition to the specific provisions contained in this Act directed toward that purpose, it is the intent of the Congress that all officers of the Government so conduct the affairs of the Government for which they exercise responsibility and authority as (1) to be mindful of problems occasioned by transitions in the office of President, (2) to take appropriate lawful steps to avoid or minimize disruptions that might be occasioned by the transfer of the executive power, and (3) otherwise to promote orderly transitions in the office of President.

H.R. 3137, A BILL TO AMEND THE PRESIDENTIAL TRANSITION ACT OF 1963

HEARING

BEFORE THE

SUBCOMMITTEE ON GOVERNMENT MANAGEMENT, INFORMATION, AND TECHNOLOGY

OF THE

COMMITTEE ON GOVERNMENT REFORM
HOUSE OF REPRESENTATIVES

ONE HUNDRED SIXTH CONGRESS

FIRST SESSION

ON

H.R. 3137

TO AMEND THE PRESIDENTIAL TRANSITION ACT OF 1963 TO PROVIDE FOR TRAINING OF INDIVIDUALS A PRESIDENT-ELECT INTENDS TO NOMINATE AS DEPARTMENT HEADS OR APPOINT TO KEY POSITIONS IN THE EXECUTIVE OFFICE OF THE PRESIDENT

OCTOBER 13, 1999

Serial No. 106–119

Printed for the use of the Committee on Government Reform

Available via the World Wide Web: http://www.gpo.gov/congress/house
http://www.house.gov/reform

U.S. GOVERNMENT PRINTING OFFICE

64–650 CC WASHINGTON : 2000

COMMITTEE ON GOVERNMENT REFORM

DAN BURTON, Indiana, *Chairman*

BENJAMIN A. GILMAN, New York
CONSTANCE A. MORELLA, Maryland
CHRISTOPHER SHAYS, Connecticut
ILEANA ROS-LEHTINEN, Florida
JOHN M. McHUGH, New York
STEPHEN HORN, California
JOHN L. MICA, Florida
THOMAS M. DAVIS, Virginia
DAVID M. McINTOSH, Indiana
MARK E. SOUDER, Indiana
JOE SCARBOROUGH, Florida
STEVEN C. LaTOURETTE, Ohio
MARSHALL "MARK" SANFORD, South Carolina
BOB BARR, Georgia
DAN MILLER, Florida
ASA HUTCHINSON, Arkansas
LEE TERRY, Nebraska
JUDY BIGGERT, Illinois
GREG WALDEN, Oregon
DOUG OSE, California
PAUL RYAN, Wisconsin
HELEN CHENOWETH, Idaho
DAVID VITTER, Louisiana

HENRY A. WAXMAN, California
TOM LANTOS, California
ROBERT E. WISE, Jr., West Virginia
MAJOR R. OWENS, New York
EDOLPHUS TOWNS, New York
PAUL E. KANJORSKI, Pennsylvania
PATSY T. MINK, Hawaii
CAROLYN B. MALONEY, New York
ELEANOR HOLMES NORTON, Washington, DC
CHAKA FATTAH, Pennsylvania
ELIJAH E. CUMMINGS, Maryland
DENNIS J. KUCINICH, Ohio
ROD R. BLAGOJEVICH, Illinois
DANNY K. DAVIS, Illinois
JOHN F. TIERNEY, Massachusetts
JIM TURNER, Texas
THOMAS H. ALLEN, Maine
HAROLD E. FORD, Jr., Tennessee
JANICE D. SCHAKOWSKY, Illinois

BERNARD SANDERS, Vermont (Independent)

KEVIN BINGER, *Staff Director*
DANIEL R. MOLL, *Deputy Staff Director*
DAVID A. KASS, *Deputy Counsel and Parliamentarian*
CARLA J. MARTIN, *Chief Clerk*
PHIL SCHILIRO, *Minority Staff Director*

SUBCOMMITTEE ON GOVERNMENT MANAGEMENT, INFORMATION, AND TECHNOLOGY

STEPHEN HORN, California, *Chairman*

JUDY BIGGERT, Illinois
THOMAS M. DAVIS, Virginia
GREG WALDEN, Oregon
DOUG OSE, California
PAUL RYAN, Wisconsin

JIM TURNER, Texas
PAUL E. KANJORSKI, Pennsylvania
MAJOR R. OWENS, New York
PATSY T. MINK, Hawaii
CAROLYN B. MALONEY, New York

EX OFFICIO

DAN BURTON, Indiana
HENRY A. WAXMAN, California

J. RUSSELL GEORGE, *Staff Director and Chief Counsel*
BONNIE HEALD, *Director of Communications/Professional Staff Member*
CHIP AHLSWEDE, *Clerk*
TREY HENDERSON, *Minority Counsel*

SERVICES AND FACILITIES AUTHORIZED TO BE PROVIDED TO PRESIDENTS-ELECT AND VICE-PRESIDENTS-ELECT

SEC. 3. (a) The Administrator of General Services, referred to hereafter in this Act as "the Administrator," is authorized to provide, upon request, to each President-elect and each Vice-President-elect, for use in connection with his preparations for the assumption of official duties as President or Vice President necessary services and facilities, including—

(1) Suitable office space appropriately equipped with furniture, furnishings, office machines and equipment, and office supplies, as determined by the Administrator, after consultation with the President-elect, the Vice-President-elect, or their designee provided for in subsection (e) of this section, at such place or places within the United States as the President-elect or Vice-President-elect shall designate;

(2) Payment of the compensation of members of office staffs designated by the President-elect or Vice-President-elect at rates determined by them not to exceed the rate provided by the Classification Act of 1949, as amended, for grade GS–18: *Provided*, That any employee of any agency of any branch of the Government may be detailed to such staffs on a reimbursable or nonreimbursable basis with the consent of the head of the agency; and while so detailed such employee shall be responsible only to the President-elect or Vice-President-elect for the performance of his duties: *Provided further*, That any employee so detailed shall continue to receive the compensation provided pursuant to law for his regular employment, and shall retain the rights and privileges of such employment without interruption. Notwithstanding any other law, persons receiving compensation as members of office staffs under this subsection, other than those detailed from agencies, shall not be held or considered to be employees of the Federal Government except for purposes of the Civil Service Retirement Act, the Federal Employees' Compensation Act, the Federal Employees' Group Life Insurance Act of 1954, and the Federal Employees Health Benefits Act of 1959;

(3) Payment of expenses for the procurement of services of experts or consultants or organizations thereof for the President-elect or Vice-President-elect, as authorized for the head of any department by section 15 of the Administrative Expenses Act of 1946, as amended (5 U.S.C. 55a), at rates not to exceed $100 per diem for individuals;

(4) Payment of travel expenses and subsistence allowances, including rental of Government or hired motor vehicles, found necessary by the President-elect or Vice-President-elect, as

authorized for persons employed intermittently or for persons serving without compensation by section 5 of the Administrative Expenses Act of 1946, as amended (5 U.S.C. 73b–2), as may be appropriate;

(5) Communications services found necessary by the President-elect or Vice-President-elect;

(6) Payment of expenses for necessary printing and binding, notwithstanding the Act of January 12, 1895, and the Act of March 1, 1919, as amended (44 U.S.C. 111);

(7) Reimbursement to the postal revenues in amounts equivalent to the postage that would otherwise be payable on mail matter referred to in subsection (d) of this section.

(b) The Administrator shall expend no funds for the provision of services and facilities under this Act in connection with any obligations incurred by the President-elect or Vice-President-elect before the day following the date of the general elections held to determine the electors of President and Vice President in accordance with title 3, United States Code, sections 1 and 2, or after the inauguration of the President-elect as President and the inauguration of the Vice-President-elect as Vice President.

(c) The terms "President-elect" and "Vice-President-elect" as used in this Act shall mean such persons as are the apparent successful candidates for the office of President and Vice President, respectively, as ascertained by the Administrator following the general elections held to determine the electors of President and Vice President in accordance with title 3, United States Code, sections 1 and 2.

(d) Each President-elect shall be entitled to conveyance within the United States and its territories and possessions of all mail matter, including airmail, sent by him in connection with his preparations for the assumption of official duties as President, and such mail matter shall be transmitted as penalty mail as provided in title 39, United States Code, section 4152. Each Vice-President-elect shall be entitled to conveyance within the United States and its territories and possessions of all mail matter, including airmail, sent by him under his written autograph signature in connection with his preparations for the assumption of official duties as Vice President.

(e) Each President-elect and Vice-President-elect may designate to the Administrator an assistant authorized to make on his behalf such designations or findings of necessity as may be required in connection with the services and facilities to be provided under this Act. Not more than 10 per centum of the total expenditures under this Act for any President-elect or Vice-President-elect may be made upon the basis of a certificate by him or the assistant designated by him pursuant to this section that such expenditures are classified and are essential to the national security, and that they accord with the provisions of subsections (a), (b), and (d) of this section.

(f) In the case where the President-elect is the incumbent President or in the case where the Vice-President-elect is the incumbent Vice President, there shall be no expenditures of funds for the provision of services and facilities to such incumbent under this Act, and any funds appropriated for such purposes shall be returned to the general funds of the Treasury.

SERVICES AND FACILITIES AUTHORIZED TO BE PROVIDED TO FORMER PRESIDENTS AND FORMER VICE PRESIDENTS

SEC. 4. The Administrator is authorized to provide, upon request, to each former President and each former Vice President, for a period not to exceed six months from the date of the expiration of his term of office as President or Vice President, for use in connection with winding up the affairs of his office, necessary services and facilities of the same general character as authorized by this Act to be provided to Presidents-elect and Vice-Presidents-elect. Any person appointed or detailed to serve a former President or former Vice President under authority of this section shall be appointed or detailed in accordance with, and shall be subject to, all of the provisions of section 3 of this Act applicable to persons appointed or detailed under authority of that section. The provisions of the Act of August 25, 1958 (72 Stat. 838; 3 U.S.C. 102, note), other than subsections (a) and (e) shall not become effective with respect to a former President until six months after the expiration of his term of office as President.

AUTHORIZATION OF APPROPRIATIONS

SEC. 5. There are hereby authorized to be appropriated to the Administrator such funds as may be necessary for carrying out the purposes of this Act but not to exceed $900,000 for any one Presidential transition, to remain available during the fiscal year in which the transition occurs and the next succeeding fiscal year. The President shall include in the budget transmitted to the Congress for each fiscal year in which his regular term of office will expire, a proposed appropriation for carrying out the purposes of this Act.

References: H.R. 4638, 88th Congress:

House Report 88-301, from Committee on Government Operations
Senate Report 88-448, from Committee on Government Operations
Conference Committee Report 88-1148

April 24, 1963 – hearings held by House Government Operations Subcommittee on Executive and Legislative Reorganization
July 25, 1963 – passed the House
October 17, 1963 – passed the Senate, with amendments
February 24, 1964 – Conference Report adopted and passed the Senate
February 25, 1964 – Conference Report adopted and passed the House
March 7, 1964 – signed into law as P.L. 88-277.

PRESIDENTIAL TRANSITION ACT OF 1963, AMENDMENTS
P.L. 94-499; OCTOBER 14, 1976; 90 STAT. 2380

Text:

An Act

To revise the appropriation authorization for the Presidential Transition Act of 1963, and for other purposes.

Be it enacted by the Senate and House of Representatives of the United States of America in Congress assembled, That (a) section 5 of the Presidential Transition Act of 1963 (3 U.S.C. 102 note) is amended to read as follows:

"SEC. 5. There are hereby authorized to be appropriated to the Administrator such funds as may be necessary for carrying out the purposes of this Act, except that with respect to any one Presidential transition—

"(1) not more than $2,000,000 may be appropriated for the purposes of providing services and facilities to the President-elect and Vice President-elect under section 3, and

"(2) not more than $1,000,000 may be appropriated for the purposes of providing services and facilities to the former President and former Vice President under section 4.

The President shall include in the budget transmitted to Congress, for each fiscal year in which his regular term of office will expire, a proposed appropriation for carrying out the purposes of this Act."

(b) Section 3(a)(3) of the Presidential Transition Act of 1963 is amended by striking out "at rates not to exceed $100 per diem for individuals".

SEC. 2. Section 3(a)(2) of the Presidential Transition Act of 1963 is amended by striking out "or nonreimbursable".

SEC. 3. The amendment made by the first section of this Act shall take effect on—

(1) the date of the enactment of this Act, or

(2) October 1, 1976,

whichever is later.

References: H.R. 14886, 94th Congress

House Report 94-1442, from the Committee on Government Operations
Senate Report 94-1322, from the Committee on Government Operations

August 4, 1976 – hearings held by House Government Operations Subcommittee on Legislation and National Security
September 1, 1976 – passed House
September 30, 1976 – passed Senate
October 14, 1976 – signed into law as P.L. 94-499.

Mr. HORN. Over the years, there have been many examples of missteps and outright errors made by newly appointed officials in the White House. However capable and well-intentioned, new and unseasoned appointees are especially susceptible to misjudgments that, at a minimum, can be politically embarrassing, but can also have serious consequences on the administration's credibility.

As we have seen, sometimes the errors tumble out in misstatements or ill-advised recommendations; other times, they have resulted in ethical lapses by an appointee who was unaware of the ethical standards required by Federal law. These errors could have been avoided if these appointees had properly understood the scope of their responsibilities, or, I might add, if they thought what this action would look like on the front page of the Washington Post or any major paper before you do it.

Accordingly, I am introducing a bill that would amend the Presidential Transition Act of 1963 to authorize the use of Presidential transition funds for a formal orientation process for incoming appointees to top White House positions, including Cabinet members. This bill would encourage the orientations to take place between the general election and 30 days after the inauguration. By establishing this timeframe for top appointee orientations, this bill would increase the likelihood that a greater number of lower-level appointees might also receive White House orientations earlier in the new administration.

[The text of H.R. 3137 follows:]

106TH CONGRESS
1ST SESSION

H. R. 3137

To amend the Presidential Transition Act of 1963 to provide for training of individuals a President-elect intends to nominate as department heads or appoint to key positions in the Executive Office of the President.

IN THE HOUSE OF REPRESENTATIVES

OCTOBER 25, 1999

MR. HORN (for himself, Mr. TURNER, Mrs. BIGGERT, Mr. KANJORSKI, and Mrs. MALONEY of New York) introduced the following bill; which was referred to the Committee on Government Reform

A BILL

To amend the Presidential Transition Act of 1963 to provide for training of individuals a President-elect intends to nominate as department heads or appoint to key positions in the Executive Office of the President.

Be it enacted by the Senate and House of Representatives of the United States of America in Congress assembled,

SECTION 1. AMENDMENTS TO PRESIDENTIAL TRANSITION ACT OF 1963.

Section 3(a) of the Presidential Transition Act of 1963 (3 U.S.C. 102 note) is amended—

(1) in the matter preceding paragraph (1) by striking "including—" and inserting "including the following:";

(2) in each of paragraphs (1) through (6) by striking the semicolon at the end and inserting a period; and

(3) by adding at the end the following:

"(8)(A) Payment of expenses during the transition for briefings, workshops, or other activities to acquaint key prospective Presidential appointees with the types of problems and challenges that most typically confront new political appointees when they make the transition from campaign and other prior activities to assuming the responsibility for governance after inauguration, including interchange with individuals who held similar leadership roles in prior administrations, agency or department experts from the Office of Management and Budget or an Office of Inspector General of an agency or department, and relevant staff from the General Accounting Office.".

"(B) Activities funded under this paragraph shall be conducted primarily for individuals the President-elect intends to nominate as department heads or appoint to key positions in the Executive Office of the President.".

○

Mr. HORN. This bill is an important step toward restoring confidence in the ability of the Executive Office of the President to run its affairs in a responsible manner.

At today's hearing, we will hear from a group of distinguished witnesses. On our first panel, we have two gentlemen who hold a unique perspective on the Presidency. We welcome Mr. Lee White, who was assistant counsel to President John F. Kennedy and counsel to President Lyndon B. Johnson; and Mr. Elliot Richardson, former Attorney General for President Richard Nixon and a holder of at least four other Cabinet positions, including Defense.

On panel two, we have Mr. Dwight Ink, former Assistant Director of the Office of Management and Budget; Mr. Paul Light, Director of the Center for Public Service at the Brookings Institute; and Mr. Norman J. Ornstein, a resident scholar at the American Enterprise Institute for Policy Research.

We welcome each of you and look forward to your testimony.

[The prepared statement of Hon. Stephen Horn follows:]

ONE HUNDRED SIXTH CONGRESS

Congress of the United States

House of Representatives

COMMITTEE ON GOVERNMENT REFORM

2157 RAYBURN HOUSE OFFICE BUILDING

WASHINGTON, DC 20515–6143

MAJORITY (202) 225-5074
MINORITY (202) 225-5051
TTY (202) 225-6852

"Presidential Transition Act Amendment of 1999"
OPENING STATEMENT
REPRESENTATIVE STEPHEN HORN (R-CA)
Chairman, Subcommittee on Government Management, Information, and Technology
October 13, 1999

A quorum being present, this hearing of the Subcommittee on Government Management, Information, and Technology will come to order.

Until 1963, the primary source of funding for presidential transitions was the incoming president's political party and the contributions of volunteer staff. The Presidential Transition Act of 1963 was enacted to authorize Federal funding and assistance for incoming Presidents. It also provided the authority for the outgoing President and Vice President to use the funds for their transition into private life for up to 6 months. The Act authorized the appropriation of $900,000 to be divided equally between the incoming and outgoing administrations.

In 1976, Congress amended the Presidential Transition Act of 1963 to increase the funding provided in the 1963 Act. In 1988, Congress passed the Presidential Transitions Effectiveness Act, which again raised the funding for presidential transitions, and included a provision that calls for annual adjustments for inflation. In addition, the 1988 Act required that all pre-election transition funds must be acquired privately, and the names of all transition personnel and private contributors are publicly disclosed.

Over the years, there have been many examples of missteps and outright errors made by newly appointed officials in the White House. However capable and well-intentioned, new and unseasoned appointees are especially susceptible to misjudgments that, at a minimum, can be politically embarrassing, but can also have serious consequences on the Administration's credibility.

As we have seen, sometimes the errors tumble out in misstatements or ill-advised recommendations; other times, they have resulted in ethical lapses by an appointee who was unaware of the ethical standards required by Federal law. These errors could have been avoided if these appointees had properly understood the scope of their responsibilities.

Accordingly, I am introducing a bill that would amend the Presidential Transition Act of 1963 to authorize the use of presidential transition funds for a formal orientation process for incoming appointees to top White House positions, including Cabinet members. This bill would encourage the orientations to take place between the General Election and 30 days after inauguration. By establishing this timeframe for top appointee orientations, this bill would increase the likelihood that a greater number of lower level appointees might also receive White House orientations earlier in the new administration. This bill is an important step toward restoring confidence in the ability of the Executive Office of the President to run its affairs in a responsible manner.

At today's hearing, we will hear from a group of distinguished witnesses. On our first panel, we have two gentlemen who hold a unique perspective on the presidency. We welcome Mr. Lee White who was assistant counsel to President John F. Kennedy and counsel to President Lyndon B. Johnson, and Mr. Elliott Richardson, former Attorney General for President Richard Nixon.

On Panel Two, we have Mr. Dwight Ink, former Assistant Director of the Office of Management and Budget; Mr. Paul Light, Director for the Center for Public Service at the Brookings Institution; and Mr. Norman J. Ornstein, a Resident Scholar at the American Enterprise Institute for Policy Research.

We welcome each of you and look forward to your testimony. I now yield to the subcommittee's Ranking Member, Mr. James Turner of Texas, for a statement.

Mr. HORN. I now yield to the subcommittee's ranking member, Mr. James Turner of Texas, for a statement.

Mr. TURNER. Thank you, Mr. Chairman. I commend you on the legislation you have brought forward. It seems to me a very good idea, and you have brought together a very distinguished panel to discuss it. Obviously anything that we can do to assist the transition of a newly elected President and his appointees and Cabinet members to make the transition smoother, we ought to do it. There have been plenty of examples, as the chairman mentioned, of cases where new appointees showed some indication that they were not quite ready for the new job that they had assumed. I think your idea here of providing an opportunity for briefings and workshops and other activities for key prospective appointees is a very good one.

I would like to thank the two panels who have come to discuss the issues with us today.

Mr. HORN. I thank the gentleman.

[Witnesses sworn.]

Mr. HORN. We will now proceed with panel one and begin with a very distinguished public servant who a lot of us have known for 20 and 30 years. The Honorable Elliot Richardson was Attorney General to President Nixon. He was Under Secretary of State, Secretary of HEW, and then Secretary of Commerce and Secretary of Defense.

Mr. Richardson, it is all yours.

STATEMENTS OF ELLIOT RICHARDSON, ATTORNEY GENERAL TO PRESIDENT NIXON; AND LEE WHITE, FORMER ASSISTANT COUNSEL TO PRESIDENT KENNEDY AND COUNSEL TO PRESIDENT JOHNSON

Mr. RICHARDSON. Thank you very much, Mr. Chairman, and members of the subcommittee. I feel not only privileged to have the opportunity to lead off the testimony in this hearing, but I also believe that it probably is one of the more important hearings that will be held in the Congress this year. It is fair to say that one would be aware of its importance only with the kind of experience one acquires through seeing the process whereby people are coming from their roles in the private sector, going to their new assignments in government, and the need for supplementation of their knowledge by as rapid as possible an exposure to the very integral kind of environment they are coming into. It is different, of course, in a whole lot of ways that I don't need to enumerate, but one is in the controversiality of many of the issues that they will address, the degree of public attention focused on them, and not the least the necessity of dealing with the legislative branch of the government, which at the end of the day has power and responsibility to dispose of the issues that are addressed by the executive branch.

There is also the relationship between the new Presidential appointees and the career services and their members who were there before the Presidential appointees arrived and will be there after they are gone.

I think these are among the reasons for the legislation that you have before you.

I was pleased to have the opportunity to read the testimony of Dwight Ink, at least the statement that he prepared, and I think that is a very comprehensive and persuasive presentation of the kinds of considerations that I have briefly touched on, and a range of other considerations which are also relevant to this legislation. I strongly support everything he has said.

I would also suggest, however, that beyond the problem which, I take it, has to be addressed through legislation for appointees of an incoming President before he takes office in order to meet the expenditures thereby entailed, that we should not lose sight of the need for the orientation and briefing of new Presidential appointees who come into office after the administration has taken over. The same considerations that apply to them due to the appointees before the administration takes office apply to the new Presidential appointees who are recruited who come in after the administration is already in place. That may not need legislation, but the considerations that do require legislation should be recognized as having continued importance, and perhaps the committee in its own report, I hope, recommending legislation for adoption with whatever modifications it may see fit to make will call attention to this second point.

The testimony of Dwight Ink, which is the only statement that I have seen, touched on a great many of the considerations which bear on the needs for this legislation. I want to stress one of them; and to that end, Mr. Chairman, I have brought with me, which I have submitted to the committee staff, a copy of a recommendation of a task force of the so-called Volcker Commission, more formally known as the National Commission on the Public Service, on which I sat in 1998. My task force addresses the relations between political appointees and career executives.

It is fair to say that not only is considerable time lost in development of a clear understanding by new appointees of the importance of this relationship, but also there is a good deal of unnecessary strain that arises out of the misunderstandings and misperceptions brought to their new posts by Presidential, which is to say political, appointees to the government insofar as their relationships with public servants of the executive branch agencies are concerned.

The word, "bureaucrat," as we all know, carries many negative connotations. It need not have negative connotations. I would advise to pretend that it doesn't deserve any negative connotations. I will emphasize, however, that a bureaucracy is any large organization requiring staff and addressing several important purposes. AT&T is a bureaucracy. IBM is a bureaucracy, and so on.

I personally regard myself as, first of all, a politician, although I seldom, I think, have been recognized as such, but I have long believed that John B. Fisher, then editor of Harvard Magazine was right when I heard him tell a Harvard audience that politics is the most difficult of the arts and the noblest of the professions. I wish not only that more members of the general public understood and believed that, but also wished that more politicians understood and believed it.

I presently do believe it, even though I think I am seldom—let me restate that. I am not often enough thought of as a politician.

Second, I regard myself as a bureaucrat with equal pride. To be a good bureaucrat, particularly as a Presidential appointee, requires that you undertake a very complex and demanding administrative job fraught also with the necessity for addressing difficult and controversial public issues. You are the head of an organization which is responsible to the policy leadership of the President under whom you serve, but also accountable to the general public through, in the first instance, contact and accountability to the Congress of the United States, but also to the general public via media, via all kinds of organizations around national and regional and local through whom the policy and purposes that you serve are communicated to the American people.

You need—in order to be able to achieve any of the public purposes of the public organizations in which you serve, and especially for those who head the organizations, you need to understand that everything you do depends at the end of the day on the people who are permanent members of the organizations of which you are a part. And you need to know that the great majority of them are people who would not be there if they were not genuinely dedicated to serving the public interest in the post that they hold. You need to presume that and proceed on that assumption, and only qualify it to the extent that in your relationships with a given individual over time, you find that assumption may not be entirely warranted.

I want to emphasize, Mr. Chairman, my first Presidential appointment was by President Eisenhower. I was Assistant Secretary for Legislation. I dealt with every committee and subcommittee of the Congress of the United States that dealt with any legislation involving health or education or welfare. There were only about five Presidential appointees in HEW in those days, maybe seven. I was No. 3 in rank order, you might say, and I served for substantial periods as Acting Under Secretary and Acting Secretary of HEW under President Eisenhower. As you pointed out, I headed four Cabinet departments and served as No. 2 in State.

I think I speak with not only firsthand knowledge, but complete realism toward the necessity for constructive relationships between Presidential appointees and media, the very real potential for those relationships. This is undercut if the Presidential appointee is a smart aleck and a cynic and stupid enough to suppose that you have to be a businessman or a Republican or a Democrat of your own basic orientation in order to be devoted to the best interests of the United States.

Presidential appointees, I am sorry to have to say, in most cases need to be made aware of that. They are becoming, you might say, officers in an institution in which there are people ready to be led who know that they need leadership in the resolution of political issues that it is not their job, they know it is not their job, to have to resolve, but who are quite ready to follow that leadership, especially if it is intelligent and articulate, and especially if the political appointees take the trouble to engage them in a process which communicates understanding of those policy decisions.

I would like to give one example going back to the Eisenhower administration which I think is very telling in this respect. There was a bill which had been introduced at that time by a senior Member of Congress from Rhode Island whose name eludes me at the moment, but it was the first piece of legislation proposing the establishment of what we now call Medicare.

I believed that the Eisenhower administration needed to have its own initiative in addressing health care needs and the financing of those needs for the elderly, so I put together a small group. There were hardly any political people in the Department at that time. We relied on career people to develop the Eisenhower administration's counterpart with a Republican slant and perspective on how to vote. This group came forward with what I thought was a not very coherent or convincing approach, and I met with them and we talked about it, and they came back with a new version which wasn't much better. And then it struck me their problem was not that they were trying to impose something that reflected their own political biases, the problem was that I had not made clear enough what were the fundamental political decisions and policies that we, the Eisenhower administration, saw as necessary to approaching that problem.

I had to do the work of singling out what these were, and the approach that I came up with was one which essentially gave in a different context we now call vouchers with which the Social Security beneficiary could buy health insurance coverage. That is enough for present purposes.

The point is that when I gave them a clear idea of what the political objectives were, then they could begin to apply it intelligently.

I came into the Nixon administration as what we now call Deputy Secretary of State. I had never had a foreign policy job before. I never worked with the Foreign Service. But one thing I learned very early on, when I saw somebody smile or look at another member of the Foreign Service around the table when we were discussing some issue with a wink, or sort of a smirk, I knew that I should ask that person a question, and if I asked a question about what they thought about what I had been saying up to that point and the direction of policy, they gave me a straight answer drawing on their knowledge and experience of the issue. They had been kicked around by enough political appointees so they didn't necessarily volunteer the answer, but if I got any clue to whatever didn't seem to be going across and asked, I got one.

The relationship between political appointees in the Department of State is very much like the relationship between political appointees and the military services. I think there is something about the uniform and the stature of the military from day one ready to speak up, but I found in those early weeks that these people were dedicated, competent professionals and very ready to take political leadership.

Now, I emphasize these things, Mr. Chairman, because the United States and the public are damaged by the wrong assumptions brought by political appointees to their positions. This is by no means the only reason why there needs to be an orientation at a transition stage, not only before an administration comes in, but for new appointees after the administration comes in.

Other reasons are spelled out in Mr. Ink's testimony, which is the only statement that I have seen. But, Mr. Chairman, I want to emphasize the point that I have emphasized because in the first place I think I have almost a unique background for having acquired the point of view I have expressed, but also because I think it is a consideration that is far too little recognized, and it is important to the success of political issues. Thank you, Mr. Chairman.

Mr. HORN. I am going to put in the record without objection the task force reports to the National Commission on the Public Service which was chaired by Mr. Volcker and the Task Force on the Relations Between Political Appointees and Career Executives which was chaired by our witness Mr. Richardson. It is a very worthwhile document, and I will put it at this point into the record.

[The information referred to follows:]

TASK FORCE REPORTS

TO THE

NATIONAL COMMISSION ON THE PUBLIC SERVICE

CHAIRMAN

Paul A. Volcker

TASK FORCES

Public Perceptions of the Public Service

Recruitment and Retention

Education and Training

Relations Between Political Appointees and Career Executives

Pay and Compensation

WASHINGTON 1989

THE TASK FORCE ON THE RELATIONS BETWEEN POLITICAL APPOINTEES AND CAREER EXECUTIVES

CHAIRMAN

Elliot L. Richardson
Former Cabinet Member

MEMBERS

Frederic V. Malek
Former Director of Presidential Personnel

Robert C. McFarlane
Former National Security Adviser

Walter F. Mondale
Former Vice President of the United States

Benjamin Read
Former Under Secretary of State for Management

Anne Wexler
Former Assistant to the President for Public Liaison

Alan Wolff
Former Deputy Special Trade Representative

PROJECT DIRECTOR

James P. Pfiffner
Professor of Government and Politics
George Mason University

RECOMMENDATION 8

The President should establish orientation programs for all new political appointees in the executive branch.

When new political appointees enter the federal government, they are often thrust into their positions with little preparation or orientation. Only 20 percent of PAS appointees from 1964 to 1984 received any orientation when they joined the government. While some new appointees have had previous government experience, 60 percent of them come from outside of the government. The orientation of new appointees should be more systematic than it has been in the past.

Appointees with backgrounds in business, the law, or academia may possess impressive expertise and experience, but the federal management context is unique in many important ways. The environment of federal organizations is dominated by Congress and the White House and is affected by the central management agencies. The internal management environment is dominated by budget, personnel, and administrative procedures that are unique to the federal government. The relationship between political appointees and career executives has few parallels in the business world. Policymaking in the federal government involves much more coordination than in most other management contexts.

But even if new appointees have worked in the federal government, they still need to learn the priorities and policy development processes of their President. Department heads need to know how the President expects them to interact with the White House staff. What are the ground rules for communicating with Congress? What role will the White House play in selecting noncareer personnel in departments and agencies?

The White House should provide an orientation program for all new PAS appointees. Recent Administrations have provided some form of orientation program for new appointees, and in the Reagan Administration the Assistant for Presidential Personnel has organized White House briefing seminars for new appointees.[44] These efforts need to be institutionalized. That is, the organization of the orientation capacity should be established in a way that will ensure its continuation across Administrations. The function could be housed in the Office of Presidential Personnel or in a permanent White House secretariat.

The persons in the office should be primarily career civil servants who will know how the sessions have been conducted in previous Administrations and who will adapt the orientations to the needs of a new Administration. This office should be responsible for developing a set of materials to which appointees can refer regarding the issues covered. The materials should include selections from relevant statutes and regulations when appropriate, for example, conflict of interest rules from the Office of Government Ethics.

Although such a unit can do the legwork, the whole program will only be effective if it has high level backing in each Administration's White House staff. Whenever possible, social functions accompanying orientation programs should include spouses of Administration officials, in order to acquaint appointees' families with the responsibilities of these offices. These programs should be set up to handle large volumes at the beginning of a new Administration and should be run on a regular basis for new appointees joining the Administration later in its tenure.

Briefing programs ought to include presentations by career executives, both to take advantage of their expertise and experience and to begin the process of acquainting new appointees with career executives with whom they will be working. It should also be emphasized that political appointees are entrusted for a short time with the management of the permanent interests of the American people and the U.S. government. This trust should not be taken lightly and should be honored so that the institutions of the government can be passed on to the next Administration in sound condition.

Senior officials are so busy in the early months of a new Administration that they find it difficult to set aside time and personnel to conduct orientation programs. Yet that is when the need is the greatest. Orientation should be assigned an early and high priority in a new Administration.

Because it is so difficult to draw busy high-level officials away from their new jobs, these orientation sessions must be conducted from the White House itself, and attendance should be mandatory. The nuts and bolts substance of the orientations should include sessions on personnel rules, budget procedures, dealing with the press, relations with Congress, and legal and ethical guidelines. They should also include briefings on the policy-development processes of the Administration as well as on the priorities of the President. The sessions can be conducted most effectively by high-level members of the Administration and by former Presidential appointees.

Orientation sessions for PAS appointees that cover agency-specific and programmatic matters should be conducted in the departments and agencies. Beginning in 1988, OPM conducted orientation sessions for noncareer members of the SES and Schedule C appointees. We endorse these programs and recommend they be institutionalized in OPM so that each new Administration can take advantage of the capacity when it takes office. The substance of the courses should be similar to the programs run in the White House.

Although career senior executives are familiar with the routine processes of the federal government, they need to be oriented to certain aspects of a new Administration. Orientation sessions should acquaint them with the personnel and policy priorities of the new Administration. The sessions should give senior executives a clear picture of the direction of the new Administration, assure them that they will be included in consideration of new policies, and reiterate that they will be expected to support actively the new Administration's policy directions. The more that career employees are involved and interact with their new political superiors, the less likely it is that suspicion and distrust will grow between the two groups.

A new President should instill a team spirit in his Administration. An ongoing program of policy briefings during an Administration can help to sustain this team spirit as well as keep officials up-to-date on Administration priorities. A President should also try to include career executives as part of the team and invite them to briefing sessions when appropriate. Joint briefing and training sessions (for example, at the Federal Executive Institute) are also useful in engendering mutual trust and smooth working relationships between career and political executives.

Mr. HORN. We deeply appreciate your sharing those experiences with us. You might be interested to know that when one of your successors, the current incumbent, as Attorney General was testifying before us in this room, I asked if she recalled Attorney General Richardson's courageous retirement when he didn't believe it was possible for him to be persuaded by the White House and interfered with by the White House and what he did. I suggested that she might want to think about that experience when the White House was pressuring her, which they have.

You have been a courageous, honest, and dedicated public servant, and our Nation is very much in your debt in this. You've been a role model for many of us, and we thank you for sharing those ideas. If you like, we are going to have Mr. White, and then we might ask a few questions. I know that you probably have a schedule of your own.

We will ask Mr. White, who has had a long experience on Capitol Hill, and who is quite knowledgeable about White House work of quite different types.

Mr. WHITE. Thank you, Mr. Chairman and Mr. Turner. Frankly this is a pretty easy assignment. I would have expected that this is already part of the law, and if it isn't, it ought to be. I certainly believe that I could work for 3 or 4 days and not find anybody who would not think that it is a good idea. It should be done, and I certainly support the concept and the legislative proposal that I have seen.

One thought that may be worth mentioning is in the language of other activities in "briefings, workshops and other activities," either in the committee report language or—I am not much on micromanaging in the bill. I should think that we should authorize development of a handbook or pamphlet or memo or whatever. One of general character for those people across the board, especially those who are going to face confirmation, but perhaps a specialized one for those people who are going into the departments and the agencies and who should know something about the problems that are there.

I was very fortunate to be part of the transition team from President Eisenhower to President Kennedy, and as you said, the statute that you are attempting to amend was adopted in 1963. In the fall of 1960, there were—I am not kidding you, there were six people working with the Eisenhower administration from the Kennedy group. There were others involved in recruiting important players, but the actual substantive involvement was a group of only six. Happily, President Eisenhower had made it clear to everybody in his administration that cooperation was required, and we got it, especially from what was then the Bureau of the Budget. Since those days things have grown as things do grow in government and elsewhere, and I can tell you that the notion of trying to have an opportunity to explore with and explain to Presidential appointees some of the pitfalls, some of the requirements and some of the ideas that they should bear in mind as they go into these new jobs is absolutely essential.

In the Kennedy White House, although the President didn't ever put it this way, we tried to make sure if anybody was ignorant, he also wasn't arrogant, because that is a terrible combination. In the

White House, I will tell you, even if you are not at the top tier, just in the middle, the kids who knew you in grade school are going to call you. I remember going home and telling my wife I must have gotten terribly, terribly bright overnight because before nobody gave a damn what I said, and now everybody wants to know what my views are. I said I wonder if it works in reverse when you leave, and the answer is yes, it does work in reverse. But it is heady stuff, and I think not only the Cabinet officers, but the White House staff has to have instruction.

It would be a good idea, if the President were so minded, to make sure that his designated Chief of Staff was the one who made this happen and that he himself could partake of it.

The pitfalls are many: ethical questions, financial disclosure. You know, that is a very important thing, but I would also urge that we go back a step and that the recruiters know some of these issues so they are not blindsiding the person who is flattered to be considered for a high position.

President Kennedy had intended to appoint a fellow to the D.C. Board of Commissioners. It was going to be a very significant one. He was going to be the first black Commissioner in the District of Columbia, Frank Reeves. Unfortunately, it came out later that Frank had forgotten to pay his income tax. Nobody had asked him if he had paid his income tax.

Now there is a checklist, I am sure, and those are the types of issues, but also you have to try to inculcate in them, especially the White House staff, what their relations are to the Cabinet. Cabinet officers get very, very testy, I can promise you, when some White House staff guy calls him up and says, the President says—he is thinking, why didn't the President call me?

That is another part of the necessary skills and judgment, and hopefully you don't make too many mistakes. We can't kid ourselves, you cannot legislate or mandate common sense and good judgment in people. What you can do is tell them some of the basic rules that you want as President, that you want followed, and hope that it will take.

One of the benefits of mankind is to profit by other people's mistakes, and so anybody who is part of this teaching team is going to be able to find a whole host of mistakes which have been made by others in the past to illustrate the point of how difficult it can be. Everybody is busy. Everybody is flattered. There are receptions around town, and you can hardly believe your good fortune to be part of a brand new administration. But people have to understand that if the President wants it, don't forget, we are here recommending that the President in his transition, the President-elect in his transition do certain things, and hopefully he will, and if it is institutionalized, there is a better chance of it happening that way.

And without wanting to beat a dead horse to death, I want to say that I do support the idea, the concept and the legislative proposal. And as I said at the outset, please let me know if anybody is opposed to it. I would like to talk to them.

Mr. HORN. You remind me of a few experiences in that point in time. I was administrative assistant to Secretary of Labor Mitchell under President Eisenhower the last year and a half, and we were involved in some of what the President wanted done in the transition, such as preservation of papers, where do they go, and so forth and so on.

I think one of the problems that I have observed in both Republican and Democratic White Houses is the younger members of the staff who go in like they are still running a campaign in both parties. I have seen it, and I think it is pathetic, shall we say. I remember one young Kennedy aide who got a lesson in executive legislative relations when he left a note on the door of a southern Congressman. He said, the President wants you to vote this way. Needless to say, Larry O'Brien heard about that and educated the young man, since Larry was one of the greatest Ambassadors from the White House to Congress in probably this century.

Mr. WHITE. He did not require a checklist of things to do. The gentleman was innately a gentleman, and crafty and smart and very obliging. I remember he called a Congressman from Nebraska and with tears in his eyes told him that they were going to close the Veterans' Administration Hospital in Lincoln, and the guy was so pleased that Larry had called him ahead of time that he almost was grateful. Can you believe that?

Mr. HORN. That is true. Courtesies are important, but I don't think that we can just worry about the high-level Presidential appointees, we need to get down into the grass roots of some of the red-hots on the campaign trail who feel that they have personally elected the President alone, and I have run into that type in both Democratic and Republican administrations.

Mr. WHITE. That may be why a little booklet would be helpful.

Mr. HORN. Plus a good talking to by people who have had positions in other administrations. I think that helps.

I want to yield time to the gentleman from Texas, Mr. Turner, the ranking member, to open with questions. It is all yours.

Mr. TURNER. I think Mr. White said it all. If this is not in the law, it should be. I found it fascinating to hear Secretary Richardson recount some of his experiences. Both of you have a wealth of knowledge in government, and I appreciate very much Secretary Richardson's reference to the fact that we need to be careful how we use the word "bureaucrat" because it is the people who have committed their entire lives to government service that really hold this place together. If we understand that partnership between the political appointees and the career public servant, I think this place can function to the benefit of the American people.

Mr. White, listening to your comments, it made me wonder if there are not some other things that we should be thinking about putting in this legislation. The period of time between a November election and the inauguration is really very short, and some of the stories that I have heard in my period of public service oftentimes shock me. I heard one story related to me by an appointee who was recounting how he was shocked to learn that he was actually the appointee to a major head of an agency of our government. The announcement came at a press conference, and he had only a brief conversation with the President about the possibility of serving. Those kinds of stories do remind us that a President-elect and transition is a very hectic time and difficult time.

As the chairman said, oftentimes those who run the campaign are not those who you would select to run the Presidency. Yet it is those people who were involved in the campaign that oftentimes are making many of the decisions.

So perhaps there are some other ideas that we should consider in this legislation, and if there are, we have a distinguished panel here, and we would certainly welcome your suggestions. I know that the chairman would.

But I really have no questions, Mr. Chairman. I have just enjoyed the depth of experience that has been shared with us.

Mr. HORN. Thank you very much.

I now yield to Mr. Ose, the gentleman from California.

Mr. OSE. Thank you, Mr. Chairman. I find myself somewhat in awe. There is not a person alive of my generation who does not know of Secretary Richardson, and I am pleased to have the opportunity to visit with Mr. White.

I think the thing that troubles me on this whole issue of transition is when I got here in January as a new Member, having come straight from business, I kind of felt like I was on the wrong end of a fire hose, and in that regard I find great merit in this transitional training idea between the November election and the January swearing in. And I am curious as to the specific criteria at the level that you both served that you find most critical to impart to the new appointees.

Mr. RICHARDSON. The most——

Mr. OSE. The most critical—when someone comes into one of these agencies, there is a whole bunch of stuff that they have to learn, and they only have 60 days roughly to learn it. What are the most critical things that those new appointees need to learn?

Mr. RICHARDSON. I think that is a good question, and I think I have an almost unique background for answering it, having had to deal with many new jobs. I ended up with 10 Presidential appointments. Some of them I held very briefly, but invariably in a new job the first thing that I came to understand is that you need to come to know as fast as you can the people you are going to be working with, including the other Presidential appointees in your department.

At the outset you may not have had a whole lot to say about it. In time you do have. But also the key thing is the career positions.

The second thing you need to know is what are the significant issues or problems that have to be addressed and what are the relative priorities in time. What do you have to resolve first, and what do you have to know in order to be able to reach either a decision or to give a recommendation to the President. And then as time permits, what are the new undertakings or recommendations or changes of direction that you may want to initiate as time goes on. That, I think, is the sequence that is relevant to any new Presidential appointment.

Once you get outside the walls of the organization to which the new appointee—in which the new appointee will be serving, you then need to look at the relationships, starting with the Congress and the committees that have most to do with the initiatives, the budget and so on, of that governmental entity. You try to make the most of the first round of contacts with the most senior people, and liaison as you can. Beyond them are the national organizations which have the greatest interest and influence on the issues you address, and whose support or opposition may be important.

And then you have to be thinking in terms of the media, the press, television and radio, both the general ones and the more specialized people who address parts of what you do.

I would like to add, Mr. Chairman and members of the subcommittee, that I am reminded by Mr. White when he talked about the relationship between new appointees and the Congress, with respect to all of these relationships, I learned one thing which I would want to emphasize to anyone coming into government. That is that you've got to understand that the person you are dealing with in a position where there is a strained relationship, even hostility perhaps, further down the road is by and large somebody like yourself but with a different job than you.

I think one of the best, most important lessons that I learned when I became the legislative assistance to the then senior Senator from Massachusetts, who was also Majority whip and chairman of Armed Services, it is amazing to think that—this was in 1953—he had only one legislative assistant. He had a chief of the office staff and one other political person on his staff, but I was the one, it turned out, who dealt with the press. One of the people that I dealt with is still around town, Rollie Evans, who later came to Congress. He was the AP reporter who covered us, and there were a number of others.

Mr. OSE. Mr. Attorney General, if I may, I wrote down those five things, the people who were also similarly appointed to yourself, for instance, in this transition; what are the significant issues or problems; what are the congressional committees with jurisdiction; what are the nongovernmental groups who have interest; and who in the media cover this issue.

Mr. White, do you share that analysis?

Mr. RICHARDSON. One quick point. Bearing in mind what I said about the press is, I assumed and found out that these guys had their own job to do, and if I simply understood that, as it turned out, there would be no problem. That is a very simple point that applies to all of these relationships. If you understand well enough, use your imagination well enough to recognize these other functions and their demands, it becomes a hell of a lot simpler.

Mr. OSE. Thank you. Mr. White.

Mr. WHITE. I would only add a couple of things. Of course I would agree with everything. I should point out that when I first met Elliot Richardson, he was administrative assistant to the senior Senator from Massachusetts. I was a legislative assistant to the junior Senator from Massachusetts, John F. Kennedy, so that is how far we go back. Elliot was always erudite then and, as you said, an icon of the way a public servant should conduct himself, and he has always been that way.

What I would add to his list, I think you have to get a good hold on who are the interest groups that you are going to meet because you are sure going to meet them. They will be there, you can bet on that.

Next, I think you ought to get to the—what is now the OMB, the old Bureau of the Budget. Those folks, I don't know if it is politicized these days, but it didn't used to be. You could really get the low-down on what is going on in any particular department and agency. So I think you ought to make that stop.

And then if you are skillful, I would think that you would find that particular character in the White House staff who you want to be your entree and establish as good a relationship as you can.

Obviously not everybody, every Cabinet or agency head is going to be able to get to the President on every issue. They have to call their shots, unless, of course—I would exclude some of the more important ones, in my view, State, Defense, the Attorney General, probably Treasury, but the Secretary of HUD doesn't normally go right smack into the President, so he ought to be able to identify who in that staff is his person.

Above all, I think you have to shake yourself a little bit. As Elliot said, this is a temporary assignment. Political appointees come and go, but the people in the agencies for the most part will be there when you get there, and they will be there when you leave, and it is very important that you know who the key people are. One of the ways to get a fix on that is to talk to your predecessor who held that job, so I would add that.

Mr. RICHARDSON. I think those are important additions. I left them out, but I totally endorse what Mr. White said.

Mr. OSE. Thank you, Mr. Chairman.

Mr. HORN. If I might add a few things to what Mr. White has said as a fellow legislative assistant just a few years after you two gentlemen, besides going to the budget examiner, which I think is what Mr. White is referring to, I regret to say that function has been politicized. In other words, Roosevelt, Truman and Eisenhower had career people, and you kept them between administrations, and they gave you a lot of good advice. I think we ought to get back to a lot of that, but that is another story. But the budget examiner is certainly one.

The people that come to see me that are Presidential appointees, I say, look, go over to GAO. There is an expert over there in that department. Take a look and they will give you a lot of studies and so forth, and then go to the Inspector General, you are going to have to deal with that person, and find out what are the key problems that everybody has shoved under the rug, and you will find that.

So I would think those are a few of the things that you might want to tack onto the list here.

Are there any questions that the gentleman has?

I thank you both for coming. We appreciate it very much, and any thoughts you have on what we can add to this bill. It is simply a draft bill. It hasn't been put in yet. I hope our Democrat colleagues and Republican colleagues will go on it. It might sound a little small, but that is OK, we make progress step by step.

I thank both of you for coming. It is a great experience to see both of you again, and we will go to panel two now.

We have Mr. Ink, Mr. Light, and Mr. Ornstein.

[Witnesses sworn.]

Mr. HORN. We will start with Mr. Ink, former Assistant Director, Office of Management and Budget in charge of General Services Administration and all sorts of things in a very valuable career in government.

We hope to get you all out of here by noon, so I think we are in pretty good shape. You have sent us very fine papers here. If you could just summarize it and don't read it.

Mr. Ink.

STATEMENTS OF DWIGHT INK, FORMER ASSISTANT DIRECTOR, OFFICE OF MANAGEMENT AND BUDGET; PAUL LIGHT, DIRECTOR, CENTER FOR PUBLIC SERVICE, BROOKINGS INSTITUTION; AND NORMAN J. ORNSTEIN, RESIDENT SCHOLAR, AMERICAN ENTERPRISE INSTITUTE FOR POLICY RESEARCH

Mr. INK. Thank you, Mr. Chairman and members of the committee. It is always a pleasure to have the opportunity to testify before this committee and particularly today on behalf of this Presidential Transition Act bill which you plan to introduce.

I believe it can improve government in two important ways. First, it can reduce costly missteps by well intentioned incoming political appointees. Second, it can improve the performance of appointees on whom a new President will have to rely in launching his or her administration. I have worked with scores of Presidential assistants over the years, and their performance certainly varies from outstanding to just plain awful.

An incoming administration brings in a number of new political appointees, as you have said, who are very able people with impressive backgrounds, but except for those who have had prior experience, almost none of them realize what awaits them in Washington. The pressures from all sides, the intrusive scrutiny that characterizes Washington, are a shock for which they are not prepared, and they find they are expected to develop new programs and legislative proposals that have to be advanced through a maze of processes and procedures with which they are not familiar. Yet time is of the essence in the first days of an administration when the opportunities are greatest.

The steep learning curve needed for these officials to get on top of their job is made more difficult because so many of them have been immersed in campaigns that are very negative toward Washington. They arrive, therefore, loathe to take advice from anyone in Washington, neither the Washington bureaucrats nor outgoing political leaders whom they feel have been captured by inside-the-Beltway creatures who have lost touch with the real America.

As a result, these new political figures, no matter how capable, are in real danger of stumbling during these first crucial weeks, not so much from what they are striving to do as from how they are functioning and their lack of familiarity with the techniques that are most likely to get things done in this complex Washington environment. These mistakes produce headlines and grist for the TV programs, and they reinforce the negative view that the public has of government.

Further, ignorance of the techniques and approaches that can best transform policy objectives into actions weakens the ability of an administration to advance the agenda on which the voters have placed it in office.

This bill would help meet the critical need for more transition attention to how incoming political leaders can manage the challenging processes of governing.

What type of subject matter to include? The bill, I think, properly leaves flexibility to a President-elect, but my written testimony does list several critical areas in which I think orientations could be especially helpful. Approaches to working effectively with Congress, for example, should be an important subject. Some incoming appointees have never read the Constitution and look down upon the Congress as simply a problem institution to deal with as little as possible, rather than as a partner in government.

Confusion over the roles of White House staff and their relationship to departments, mentioned in the prior panel, is another area in which new administrations tend to flounder at first and another subject to be included.

An area that is perhaps least understood by new political appointees is one which Elliot Richardson talked about at some length. That is the value of the career service and how to provide it with positive leadership, a gap in knowledge that can be very costly. The career leadership is a tremendous and indispensable resource of incoming political appointees, but it needs to have positive leadership.

Although orientations are not going to reduce the conflicting pressures, the number of pressure groups, or the incessant scrutiny that characterizes Washington, they can be of great help in preparing new appointees to cope with these circumstances.

Finally, as to style, I would certainly hope that the orientations authorized by this bill would be organized much more as informal discussions and workshops with particular emphasis on involving those who have served in these kinds of positions in prior administrations, and not as lectures or briefings.

In conclusion, Mr. Chairman, I think there are many things that can be done to help improve the Presidency. I think the work that Norm Ornstein and his organization are doing and that of Paul Light and the Center for the Study of the Presidency may provide grist for this committee to consider other legislative suggestions.

I think this bill deserves strong bipartisan support as one of those steps that can make the American Presidency more effective in the 21st century. Thank you.

Mr. HORN. Thank you very much. That is a very thorough document that you have presented, and we appreciate it.

[The prepared statement of Mr. Ink follows:]

TESTIMONY OF DWIGHT INK

BEFORE THE

SUBCOMMITTEE ON GOVERNMENT MANAGEMENT,

INFORMATION AND TECHNOLOGY

HEARINGS ON

TRANSITION ORIENTATION FOR KEY POLITICAL APPOINTEES

OCTOBER 13, 1999

Testimony of Dwight Ink
Before the
House Subcommittee on
Government Management, Information and Technology

TRANSITION ORIENTATIONS

Mr. Chairman and Members of the Committee:

I am pleased to have the opportunity to testify on behalf of a bill that would amend the Presidential Transition Act to authorize transition orientation for individuals the president-elect intends to appoint to positions in the cabinet and the Executive Office of the President.

Avoidable missteps by well-intentioned political appointees of incoming administrations can be damaging and often undercut the momentum which new presidents must have to quickly launch new initiatives when the opportunities are greatest. Equally unfortunate are instances in which new appointees fall short of their potential performance because of failure to understand basics of how to get things done in the complicated world of Washington.

I believe passage of this bill would reduce some of these early problems, and could increase the early effectiveness of a new presidency. All of the former political appointees from both parties with whom I have discussed this concept believe that transition orientations would be useful as a new administration prepares to take office.

What are the types of problems this legislation would help solve?

PROBLEM

Accompanied by considerable publicity, an incoming administration brings in a number of new political appointees, many of whom are very able people with impressive

64-650 99 - 2

backgrounds. They come to the nation's capital both mission-minded and in a hurry to make changes and to pursue new policy initiatives.

But, except for those who have served here in the past, almost none of them fully realize what awaits them in Washington. Their new environment is very different from what most of them have seen in their prior business or other professional life, even those from state and local government. They lack the experience that would prepare them for the complexity of national government, the economic and political power of myriad special interest groups whose big guns are focused on Washington, and the level of intense daily scrutiny to which they will be subjected.

Many have been immersed only weeks before in campaigns that have become increasingly negative about Washington. They arrive, therefore, loathe to listen to advice from either Washington career "bureaucrats" or outgoing political appointees whom they distrust as representing the other party or believe have become captured by those "inside-the-beltway" creatures who have lost touch with the real America. In fact, even their level of confidence in outgoing officials from an administration of the same party tends to be surprisingly low.

As a result, new political executive, however capable and well-intentioned, are in danger of stumbling during the first crucial weeks and months of an administration, not so much from **what** they are striving to do but from **how** they are functioning and lack of familiarity with techniques that are most likely to achieve policy goals in a complex Washington environment. Most of these stumbles produce headlines and grist for TV news reporters and commentators for days and weeks, causing grief to the president who called them here and reinforcing the negative view the public has of government.

Even when they do not stumble, those new to the Washington scene have a good deal to learn about how to get things done in this new setting. They face an extremely steep learning curve, one that needs to begin during the transition.

TRANSITION NEEDS

Most transition efforts have included preparation of numerous briefing papers and books about the status of existing programs and problems as perceived by the outgoing administration. Task forces are established to help translate campaign rhetoric into realistic new initiatives and proposed legislation. Some of these efforts are quite useful, but little is included about how Washington works. Not much is mentioned about the operational minefields facing a new presidency and how they might be overcome. Briefing books are not the right vehicle for helping incoming political leadership learn how to avoid the pitfalls of a new presidency or providing suggestions on how a presidency can function effectively. Neither are the transition task forces and teams helpful for those purposes, despite their usefulness in the policy areas.

This bill could help meet the critical need for more transition attention to how incoming political leaders can effectively manage the challenging processes of governing in this new environment.

Congressional Relations. Just what kind of subject matter might be considered in this new direction?

Traditional transition activities fail to include much, for example, about how the top political leadership of an incoming administration can most effectively work with Congress in the crucial days just before and after inauguration. Yet, the constitutional role of the Congress is little understood by most new political appointees, and they fail to place this critical area very high on their priority list of urgent matters to address.

Because Congress is an unwieldy body, at times hostile to administration initiatives, the notion of investing precious time in cultivating these relationships, particularly with leaders of the opposition party, is repugnant. Yet its 535 members, roughly 300 committees and subcommittees, plus thousands of staff, will determine the funds and nature of the programs within which a new administration can move its agenda forward. Early mistakes in handling relations with Congress, particularly those that create distrust, will delay consideration of administration legislative initiatives and generate an unnecessary level of opposition leading to hostile hearings and crippling amendments.

I believe these missteps could be reduced, and the initial batting average of a new president's legislative proposals could be improved, if top political appointees were to spend time during the transition talking informally with people from both parties who occupied similar positions successfully in prior administrations and who, as part of an orientation program, would share their experience in working with congress. Past mistakes in working with congress can be as illuminating as successes. The perspectives of scholars who have studied the respective roles of the presidency and congress could also be of help, though lectures are not likely to be effective in this setting. In addition, I would urge the inclusion of several members of congress from both parties in this portion of orientation discussions.

White House Staff. Modern presidents increasingly use their personal White House staffs in every phase of policy coordination and development. Most senior staff are designated prior to inauguration, but there are only a few weeks at most between designation and assumption of their responsibilities in the pressure cooker environment of a new presidency. Few have the advantage of prior White House experience, and some of the most able designees have almost no relevant credentials other than knowing the president-elect or having been useful in campaign activities. As they take up their important roles as chiefs of staff and top presidential assistants in the hectic days following inauguration, they risk advancing recommendations that are not thought out or coordinated, making ill-advised statements to the press, and failing to recognize the ethical standards they will be expected to meet and how those differ from the private sector. Caught by surprise in unfamiliar terrain, inexperienced staff can quickly precipitate a minor White House crisis with the mishandling of press and congressional inquiries.

Understanding the constructive role that should be played by White House staff, and their relationship with those who head departments and agencies, can do much before and after inauguration to help develop the early cooperation and teamwork required within a new administration to develop successful policies and legislative proposals.

Conversely, an arrogant or stumbling and disorganized White House will add to the costly internal confusion and bickering that undermine effective executive leadership at times. A transition orientation program that includes candid discussions with former incumbents about techniques and behavior that have had both positive and negative results in the past could be of great help during this critical juncture. Drawing upon this reservoir of past experience also provides a more solid footing for innovation and new approaches.

Executive Office Officials. Crucial as the White House staff members are, a much larger number of people work in other units of the Executive Office of the President, such as the Office of Management and Budget which is a very powerful entity. They also represent the president and are in constant contact with the various departments and agencies, the Congress, and external groups. How the new leaders in these organizations approach their work is of utmost importance to the functioning of a new administration.

Executive Office officials need orientation discussions during the transition, because along with the White House staff, they need to hit the ground running. And, as with White House staff, these political leaders simply do not have the time for orientation discussions in the midst of pressures that beset them from all sides in the first weeks following inauguration, the time when they are most vulnerable to costly errors.

Role of Career Service. Failure to recognize the value of the 1.7 million men and women in the career service is a particularly common characteristic of incoming political appointees. No president or cabinet member can reach their program goals and deliver those programs to the public effectively without the career service, but a substantial number of appointees enter their positions with negative perceptions, ranging from disdain to hostility, of the career men and women they inherit.

Rarely, if ever, do business executives take over new firms openly expressing views of the employees they are about to lead that are as derogatory as those we find to be common among new political appointees. Blanket indictments of the Washington "bureaucrats" are common. Yet, dealing at arms length with the career service and with little effort to provide leadership or understanding of the goals of the new administration. these new appointees nonetheless have to depend upon career people to implement these new policy goals. By excluding the career people from meaningful discussions about the new initiatives, and limiting their participation in planning implementation actions, much of the value of the career experience is lost. Equally important, they do not develop a sense of ownership in the success of the new policies that they might otherwise have. A president-elect must depend upon the White House staff and cabinet to provide the positive leadership and outreach to the career service that is needed, a task for which many are not prepared.

New appointees can gain a better perspective of the career service from those political leaders who learned in prior years how valuable most career men and women are and found successful approaches in leading them to carry out presidential policies effectively. Understanding the career service is another dimension missing from most transitions, and it is a highly appropriate subject for the type of orientations this bill would authorize.

External Pressures. Few incoming appointees are prepared for the pervasive pressure exerted by special interest groups skilled in generating publicity and motivating congressional advocates to influence executive actions. An estimated 20,000 nation-wide, interest groups with their headquarters in Washington have frustrated many new political appointees beyond their capacity to function effectively. Special issue campaigns directed at Washington office-holders in charge of the targeted programs can be very stressful and time-consuming. Few are prepared for this onslaught.

Similarly, incoming political appointees are rarely prepared for the potential impact of an aggressive investigative press or the role of inspectors general and the General Accounting Office. They encounter a level of sustained external scrutiny far beyond that which they experienced in the private sector or in most state and local government positions. Some of this scrutiny will appear extremely intrusive and unfair. Even in the absence of scandal, this oversight can divert huge chunks of valuable time and energy from the urgent business of launching a new presidency. The instinctive defensive stance and stonewalling actions of the uninitiated are counter-productive, often escalating public relations molehills into mountains.

Advance tips on how to deal with these circumstances will not remove them, but orientations that provide early suggestions from those who have dealt successfully with similar challenges in the past should help the new officials to cope more effectively.

IS LEGISLATION NECESSARY?

There is no existing law that clearly prohibits the use of transition funds for orientation. So why pass another law? I would advance several reasons:

- **Legal Uncertainty.** In the absence of congressional authorization, there is uncertainty in the minds of some as to whether transition funds can be used for orientations, resulting in a natural inclination to defer such programs until after inauguration. At that point, the new responsibilities of governance make it unlikely that meaningful top-level orientations will take place at all.

- **Competition for Attention.** The transition team of a president-elect faces a range of important activities for which there is little time to plan or execute. Campaign rhetoric has to be reformulated into realistic governance policies. Programs need to be developed that are consistent with campaign promises, but can be funded, a process that gives many new people a rude awakening as they learn more about the federal budget.

  The sorting out of people who can best fill key political posts in the new administration is a daunting task, with a number of the least qualified jockeying hardest for positions. Many who were most effective in organizing campaign rallies and writing attention-getting press releases are ill-equipped for moving from campaign to governance, thereby creating tension and some confusion at a point when generating teamwork is of critical importance. All this time, the press is digging diligently for scraps of information about people who may end up in these key roles and scrambling for tidbits about rumored new initiatives that may not even be under serious consideration.

In this frantic environment, at times bordering on chaos, it is not easy for orientation activities to compete for attention. A congressional imprimatur such as this bill would provide should help orientations gain a place on the crowded transition schedule.

- **Avoid Congressional Criticism.** There are some who fear that attempts to better equip prospective appointees to fulfill their future responsibilities could be offensive to members of congress who might regard such activities as assuming Senate confirmation before the Senate acts. I do not believe that congress would regard orientations as weakening the Senate role in any way. To the contrary, I should think that senators holding confirmation hearings would prefer that a president forward the names of people who understand the responsibilities they are about to undertake and how to function effectively.

- **Facilitate Lower Level Orientations.** If orientation of top White House staff and cabinet members takes place during the transition, I believe an administration would move much more quickly after inauguration to ensure orientation of the rest of the 3,000 political employees using regular agency appropriations, a process that is now hit and miss. Currently, such programs actions may not be conducted until a presidency has been underway for several years and a series of easily avoided scandals and damaging missteps has occurred.

WHAT TYPE OF ORIENTATION?

I am pleased that the bill does not spell out the details of what the orientations should be. A president-elect should have flexibility in tailoring them to the circumstances at that time and his or her particular needs.

I do, however, support the language that requires at least a portion of the orientation to involve an "interchange with individuals who held similar leadership roles in prior administrations." I believe they can offer more practical suggestions, and enjoy greater credibility, than anyone else concerning the types of operating problems the new leaders are most likely to encounter, as well as describe techniques that have been useful in coping with them.

Other than this requirement, the bill permits each administration to utilize its own format for the orientations. One approach, for example, might include individual sessions for each of four or five major topics, such as congressional relations, the role of White House staff, interaction of the White House staff with departments and agencies, and the operation of the National Security Council and the Office of Management and Budget.

Early orientation of prospective White House staff is an essential component of transition orientations. Under this approach, those who the president-elect is seriously considering for top political positions, even though the exact titles and assignments may not have been determined for some, would meet with former White House appointees held in high regard from three or more prior administrations of both parties. These sessions would be informal with issues identified more to stimulate discussion than to serve as a fixed agenda. In this formulation, the sessions would be interactive, with introductory statements rather than briefings. Indepth discussions would be designed to encourage participants to think through how they might cope with the practical operational problems typically encountered in the position they are about to occupy.

The fact that such sessions are to be held should be public information, but probably not publicized. To ensure candor, the sessions would not be open to observers. A nonpartisan institution, or a combination of several with experience in the field, may be useful in assisting the president-elect and his staff in organizing the orientation sessions. But I would caution against a large effort under contract, which could easily become too formal and over-structured. Further, I believe volunteer efforts could hold the costs of this initial phase of high-level transition orientations to a very modest level.

Post-transition orientations involving the far larger number of political employees that utilize the usual agency appropriations and authorities, would be a different story. That second more extensive phase after inauguration will require much more in the way of organization and funds. Stronger early leadership by the incoming administration than we have seen in the past is vital for this later effort to be effective.

Clearly, there are limits to what this bill can accomplish. For example, orientations authorized by this bill will be handicapped by the fact that some of the key political posts may not be chosen until just before inauguration, too late to participate. Further, the effectiveness of these orientations will vary according to the support they receive from the president-elect. And no amount of orientation will compensate for unqualified appointees.

SUMMARY

In summary, I welcome the interest of the Chairman and the Committee in making presidential transitions more effective. There is now a lot to be desired in how some transitions are planned and executed. It is in the interest of all Americans that a new administration voted into office is able to advance its agenda for congressional and public review as quickly and effectively as possible.

There are many efforts underway by several organizations to help the next presidency operate effectively. The Pew Foundation, for example, has provided funding to several excellent organizations that have the capacity to help the next president. The Center for the Study of the Presidency, under the new leadership of Ambassador David Abshire, is planning a number of events culminating in a report to the next president on presidential leadership that will address the whole presidential term, not just the transition period.

The results of these efforts may suggest additional legislation this Committee will want to consider in the future. In the meantime, I believe the orientation bill you have under consideration deserves strong bipartisan support as one of the steps needed to make our presidency even more effective in the 21st century.

Mr. HORN. Next is one of my favorite authors, Dr. Paul Light, and I urge anyone who thinks that we don't have problems to read Thickening Government. Those in the Eisenhower administration, as a number of us were in this room, it is just unbelievable the royal titles that have been added on, Councilor to the Secretary, it is like Bismarck had been reincarnated in America. I must say, the legislative assistant is bad enough. It is now called the legislative director, and there are numerous legislative assistants, and I think we got just as much done in those days as they are getting done now with five more people.

Mr. LIGHT. It is a pleasure to testify before one of my favorite readers; one of my few readers, I might add.

The last time I was here, we were talking about raising the President's salary, and a particularly nasty conversation with a colleague from another perspective, but you got that done, and congratulations to this subcommittee for being the engine of a rather significant amount of reform in these past years. It is rather quite remarkable what the chairman and the members of this committee have been able to accomplish. I look now on this subcommittee as a real treasure for actually producing meaningful reform in relatively small bites, but you show the value of making those small steps, and they add up.

Mr. HORN. We had good bipartisan support.

Mr. LIGHT. I wish I could have given your e-mail address rather than mine in the wake of raising the President's salary because I got a ton of e-mail from people who thought that was not necessarily the best idea of all time. It was a good idea, and I am glad that you were able to do it. I mean, I am obligated whenever I testify with Dwight Ink to endorse whatever Dwight Ink says. It is part of the obligation that I have, and this is an easy one to do. The National Academy of Public Administration has long supported this idea. The Volcker Commission has supported it. Al Gore and National Performance Review had buried in one of their appendices in their first report in 1993 an endorsement of this idea. They didn't do anything about it even though the vice president could have, I suspect, persuaded the President to institute an orientation program. It was not done. The Council for Excellence in Government does do orientations now. They have some private funding to do so, and the Pew Charitable Trust, which has funded Norm Ornstein's project and mine, did include in our grant some funds to do orientation. We would be delighted to have the orientation adopted as an ongoing responsibility of government.

As you know, in the statement I can't resist an opportunity to expand an idea, no matter how good. My concern about this bill is simply that if you are going to open up the Presidential Transition Act of 1963, perhaps we can add one or two ideas to that legislation that would address other issues that I think we have broad general agreement need to be fixed.

My general point in the statement is that the Presidential appointments process as it is currently operating today is teetering on the edge, if not completely broken. We are not generating appointments in a timely fashion. We have more vacancies now in this administration than I daresay existed in Disney World during Hurricane Floyd. We are in a situation now where we do not make timely appointments. The Senate is unable to discharge its responsibilities in a timely fashion, and I think it is fair to argue that no matter how good the orientation program might be that this subcommittee would design and produce, and no matter how good it would be actually implemented, we are now in a situation where there are serious problems with the appointments process. No appointees equals no value from an orientation program.

I summarize the role of citizen service by invoking Thomas Jefferson's tremendous commitment to the notion that all citizens are obligated to serve, but in reality we are seeing increases in vacancy rates, increases in delays, increases in refusals to accept appointment, and an increase in departures. There is no question that the thickening of government has something to do with it, a small piece to do with it. Pay has something to do with it. The general climate in this country toward service has something to do with it.

We are working now as part of the Presidential Service Initiative at Brookings in collaboration with other organizations and in partnership with others who are working on this issue to generate meaningful pragmatic bipartisan ideas for reform, and we will be bringing those forward in the future.

However, I cannot resist remembering being in this room in 1988 when the Senate Governmental Affairs Committee and the House Government Operations Committee were debating the 1988 Presidential Transitions Effectiveness Act. As you know, most of these kinds of conferences are staff-driven, but a gentleman who is remembered through this painting to my left and your right entered this room through that door to argue against, and reasonably argue against, the notion of providing a little bit of preelection transition planning support for the two major party committees, and we dropped that provision.

It had bipartisan unanimous support from the Senate. We could not make the case here in this Chamber. Certainly it was a thin reed on which to make the case that giving the parties $250,000 each to do a little bit of advance planning in the preelection period might improve the odds that they could get their appointees in place in time so they could take advantage of this wonderful idea for an orientation program that this subcommittee is now considering.

I strongly urge the subcommittee to take another look at that provision. It is a tiny amount of money, a mere pile of balloons that we could easily take out of the funding that we are giving the two national party committees to host their conventions next summer. It is a nice little idea. I haven't asked Dwight how he feels about it.

Mr. INK. I support the idea. I think there are a number of things that can be done in addition to this. I just—this is one that I thought would have bipartisan support that we could probably get passed rather easily.

Mr. LIGHT. These are good little ideas for improving the odds that the next administration, be it Democrat or Republican, will hit the ground running, and we have examples from past history of administrations that have hit the ground going backward and that have hit the ground going forwards. And I think the model transition is the 1980 Reagan administration, which is clearly a product of thoughtful preelection transition planning and the courage of a Presidential candidate that said, I am going to be governing if I am elected, and I need to start planning today. Whether this subcommittee needs to get in the business of telling candidates to do that is a judgment call, but I would be remiss if I didn't take advantage of this opportunity to thicken the legislative agenda.

Thank you.

[The prepared statement of Mr. Light follows:]

ORIENTING THE PRESIDENT'S APPOINTEES

TESTIMONY BEFORE THE UNITED STATES HOUSE OF REPRESENTATIVES SUBCOMMITTEE ON MANAGEMENT, INFORMATION, AND TECHNOLOGY

PAUL C. LIGHT

THE BROOKINGS INSTITUTION

OCTOBER 13, 1999

It is a pleasure to appear before this subcommittee to endorse yet another good idea from Dwight Ink for improving the governance of this nation. It is admittedly a small idea, one that will be barely noticed in the chaos of ideas and appointments that will occupy Congress and the next president in the first months of 2001.

But it also happens to be a good idea, one that past presidential appointees have endorsed as a critical need, and one that will help the next administration move more quickly to govern the federal establishment. Those who have been involved in management reform for a while quickly realize that it is often small ideas that make the greatest difference in the long term. I believe this is just such an idea and wholeheartedly encourage the subcommittee to move quickly toward passage.

I would be remiss, however, if I did not encourage this subcommittee to go much further in addressing the fundamental problems in the presidential appointments process. I think it is fair to argue that the presidential appointments process is now on the verge of complete collapse. Absent immediate action to fix the process by which this nation appoints its citizen leaders, there will be little need for orientation. We are already governing with what I believe to be the largest number of acting appointees in American history, none of whom would qualify for orientation under even the broadest application of the definitions embedded in Dwight Ink's proposal, and I see no reason to believe that the next administration, whether led by a Democrat or Republican, will be more successful moving nominations forward. Every administration since 1960 has been later than its predecessor in appointing its leaders; there is no reason to expect a change in 2001.

Problem Statement

Let me start my assessment of the presidential appointments process with a simple point: American government was designed to be led by citizens who would step out of private life for a term of office, then return to their communities enriched by service and ready to recruit the next generation of citizen servants. The Founding Fathers believed in a democracy led by individuals who would not become so enamored of power and addicted to perquisites that they would use government as an instrument of self-aggrandizement. They fully understood that the qualities of a president's appointments were as important to the public's confidence as the laws that its elected leaders would enact. "There is nothing I am so anxious about as good nominations," Thomas Jefferson wrote at the dawn of his presidency in 1801, "conscious that the merit as well as reputation of an administration depends as much on that as on its measures."

The Founders themselves modeled their vision of citizen service by accepting the first presidential appointments, leaving behind their farms, businesses, and law practices to accept their country's call. For many, presidential service was the least of their accomplishments. They accepted the call as an obligation of citizenship. Indeed, Jefferson did not even list his ascension to the Presidency on his epitaph. He believed his greatest service to the nation was in creating the University of Virginia.

Two hundred years later, the Founders' model of citizen service is under duress as more and more of the nation's most talented leaders reject the call to lead. Presidential recruiters report a rising tide of turndowns as they begin the recruiting process. The problems are particularly visible at the start of each presidential administration where the process for entering office has become an obstacle course of isolation. endless review, personal expense, and unrelenting media scrutiny. Those who survive the process enter office frustrated and fatigued, in part because they so often endure the process with little or no help, and in part because the process has become an almost insurmountable obstacle course.

All totaled, the next president will make more than 6,000 appointments in his or her first term, including roughly 600 Senate-confirmed cabinet and subcabinet members, another 600 noncareer members of the Senior Executive Service, and 1,500 personal and confidential assistants exempted from the merit system under Schedule C of the civil service code. He or she will also appoint several hundred federal judges, and several thousand members of advisory boards, commissions, and special councils. Building a presidential administration today is equivalent to creating an executive search firm on day one and recruiting the leadership for an organization staffed by 1.8 million employees within the next 74 days, which is incidentally exactly the number of days between the next presidential election on November 7, 2000 and the inaugural on January 20, 2001.

Even if the next administration gets moving quickly, the costs of service have risen to the point that presidential headhunters report an alarming increase in the number of refusals as they start the process of selecting actual candidates.[1] Appointees report increasing frustration filling out the forms, scheduling the key meetings, and surviving the Senate confirmation process.[2]

The forms themselves are a briar patch of complexity as the Office of Presidential Personnel (White House), Office of Government Ethics (Justice Department), Federal Bureau of Investigation, the separate departments and agencies, and Senate committees collect often needless information. All but the most minor appointees must fill out Form SF 86, "Security Investigation Data for Sensitive Position" listing every residence they have occupied since January 1, 1937, and every last one must fill out Form SF-278, "Executive Personnel Financial Disclosure Report," a form so complicated that it carries a 17-page instruction sheet complete with two pages simply defining terms. One needs only read the first paragraph of the general instructions to sense the complexity:

---

[1]These concerns were first raised in an off-the-record conference of presidential recruiters hosted by the National Academy of Public Administration in 1984, and reflect ongoing conversations with headhunters since; see National Academy of Public Administration, *Recruiting Presidential Appointees: A Conference of Former Presidential Personnel Assistants* (Washington, D.C.: National Academy of Public Administration 1984).

[2]See, for example, *Obstacle Course: The Report of the Twentieth Century Fund Task Force on the Presidential Appointment Process* (New York: Twentieth Century Fund Press, 1996).

This form consists of the front page and four Schedules. You must complete each Part of all Schedules as required. If you have no information to report in any Part of a Schedule, you should indicate "None." If you are not required to complete Schedule B or Part II of Schedule D, you should leave it blank. Schedule A combines a report of income items with the disclosure of certain property interests. Schedule B deals with transactions in real property or certain other assets, as well as gifts and reimbursements. Schedules C and D relate to liabilities and employment relationships. After completing the first page and each Part of the Schedules (including extra sheets of any Schedule where continuation pages are required for any Part), consecutively number all pages.

Most appointees must also fill out the White House Personal Data Statement Questionnaire, the Internal Revenue Service Tax Check Waiver, the White House Permission for FBI Investigation, and the White House Consent Form for Nomination. And all Senate-confirmed appointees must fill out entirely separate forms for their respective committees, almost none of which fit the categories defined by the White House or SF-278, and almost all of which change from year to year as new committee members come and go. Although the forms are burdensome for everyone, they are particularly painful for appointees to advisory committees, volunteer boards, and blue-ribbon commissions where service is part-time and remuneration nonexistent.

Together, the sheer number of jobs to fill and rising tide of paperwork have contributed to five basic problems with the presidential appointments process today.

1. *Vacancy rates are rising.*

At the start of President Clinton's second term in the spring of 1997, nearly 250 or a third of the government's 725 top jobs were vacant. Although the number came down as the year wore on, vacancy rates now average roughly 25 percent per year. During 1998, for example, the Federal Election Commission was unable to hold a quorum to do its job monitoring election finance, while the Food and Drug Administration operated without a commissioner for 18 straight months until last year.

2. *Delays are increasing.*

The length of time required to fill the top jobs has been rising steadily over the past thirty years. The average appointee in the Kennedy administration was confirmed 2.4 months after the inauguration; the average appointee in the Clinton administration was confirmed in 8.5 months. If current trends hold, it will take the next president between 11 and 12 months to get his or her cabinet into office. The delays are not reserved just for executive branch posts. From 1996 to the present, it has taken President Clinton an average of 618 days to nominate a candidate for a judicial vacancy. As President Clinton complained a year into his first term, "I think, frankly, the process takes too long now. I have talked to several Republicans and Democrats who have no particular axe to grind now who think maybe it's time to have a bipartisan look at this whole appointments process. It takes took long to get somebody confirmed. It's too bureaucratic. You have two and three levels of investigation. I think it's excessive."[3]

3. *Talented Americans appear to be opting out.*

Presidential recruiters interviewed as part of the proposal development effort report two parallel trends in the appointments process.[4] The first is an increase in *turndowns* by people who have been approached for an initial review. The second is an increase in the number of *reversals* by candidates who accept a nomination, but eventually withdraw due to delays or costs. The result is that merely identifying someone willing to endure the process takes more time, increasing the delays between the opening of an administration and the actual nomination of candidates for positions. Hence, the growing vacancy rate discussed above. Although good people are still coming into government, the anecdotal evidence suggests that presidents are "drafting" from fifth, sixth, and seventh rounds instead of the first, second, and third. As David Gergen wrote in 1991, "If the nation is to restore a measure of civility and common purpose in meeting its domestic crises, it must find ways to end the relentless, ugly assaults upon the character of its public figures."[5] It is little wonder that talented people would opt out of a system that exposes every detail of their lives to the fullest public scrutiny, or that they might be frightened off by the White House's own questionnaire that asks whether they "have ever had any association with any person, group, or business venture that could be used, even unfairly, to impugn or attack your character and qualifications for a government position?"[6]

4. *Turnover is rising.*

Burned out by the process of entering office, appointees appear to be leaving office faster. A 1994 report by the General Accounting Office showed that the average length of service between 1981 and 1991 for appointees without fixed terms was only 2.1 years. Other data confirm the pattern. The Federal Aviation Administration has had seven appointed and 4 acting administrators over the past 15 years; the Federal

---

[3]Remarks on *Larry King Live*, January 20, 1994.

[4]These trends were highlighted at a recent luncheon conversation involving E. Pendelton James, headhunter to President Reagan, Constance Horner, headhunter to President Bush, and Lloyd Cutler, White House Counsel to President Clinton, and have become part of the accepted, if undocumented, wisdom regarding the current process.

[5]David Gergen, "How to Improve the Process," *U.S. News & World Report*, October 28, 1991, p. 39.

[6]White House Personal Data Statement Questionnaire, question number 41.

Housing Administration has had 13 commissioners over the past 14 years; and the General Services Administration has had 18 administrators over the past 24 years.

5. *Most importantly perhaps, the process is becoming increasingly abusive to those who decide to serve.*

Nominees report that the euphoria of being called to service is quickly replaced by the twin emotions of uncertainty and isolation.[7] Once the forms are turned in, the FBI field investigation and confirmation process can last a half year or more under the best of circumstances, and often generates intensive, frequently partisan and hostile investigation of nominees. No other institution in American society is so cavalier or cruel in its treatment of the very people it seeks as its leaders. Fears of making a bad appointment have created such anxiety that high level appointments are delayed for months as names are vetted. The White House that vetted Janet Reno's nomination as Attorney General is reported to have made 200 phone calls digging relentlessly into any hint of scandal.[8]

The Founders most certainly expected the time spent in citizen service to be inconvenient, even burdensome. That was part of the obligation to serve. "In a virtuous government," Jefferson wrote, "public offices are what they should be: burdens to those appointed to them, which it would be wrong to decline, though forseen to bring with them intense labor and private loss."

So noted, they did not expect the process of entering office to exact such delay and frustration. They clearly wanted presidents to make speedy nominations and the Senate to discharge its advice-and-consent function, aye or nay, with equal dispatch. Two hundred years later, it is safe to argue that the presidential appointments process is increasingly incapable of fulfilling its most basic responsibility: recruiting talented citizens for government service. More and more citizens are saying no, and those that do say yes are being forced through a process that is more torturous than the Founders ever could have imagined.

A Simple Idea

There are many ways to fix the presidential appointments process, not all of which need be funded by the federal government. I should note that The Pew Charitable Trusts only recently

---

[7]See, for example, the survey results reported in G. Calvin Mackenzie, ***The In-and-Outers: Presidential Appointees and Transient Government in Washington*** (Baltimore: Johns Hopkins University Press, 1987), which reports on the last comprehensive survey of presidential appointees.

[8]Burt Solomon, "The True Secrets of Clintonite...Linger Behind the 'Vetting' Veil," *National Journal*, March 13, 1993, p. 39.

provided a $3.6 million grant to the Brookings Institution to create the Presidential Service Initiative as a bipartisan source of help for future appointees.[9]

The Initiative, which will be guided by an impeccably bipartisan advisory board and staff, is designed primarily to encourage talented Americans to accept the call to service by easing the burdens of entering office in two ways. The first is to help appointees navigate the current process by providing information on everything from filling out the forms to getting started in office. Suffice it to note that being a presidential nominee today, no matter how important the job, is akin to becoming the Maytag repairman--no one is there to help the nominee through the process, except, that is, for high-priced lawyers and accountants. The second is to make the process itself more hospitable for future appointees by focusing on a set of pragmatic, noncontroversial reforms that would make the forms easier to complete, the process smoother, and entry into office faster.

Although much of the research that will guide the Presidential Service Initiative reform agenda is yet to be done, I feel comfortable recommending one simple idea to this subcommittee, if only because it is an idea that I have advocated for the better part of the 15 years, first in my role Director of Governmental Studies at the National Academy of Public Administration, where we first inventoried the now-familiar list of problems described above, then as a senior advisor to the Senate Governmental Studies Committee, where I helped draft the legislative report underpinning the Presidential Transitions Effectiveness Act of 1988.

Simply and emphatically stated, I strongly recommend that Congress provide modest funding for pre-election transition planning by the two major national parties--modest meaning no more than $250,000 to each party. That planning would give the next administration a running start at making nominations, which in turn would accelerate the confirmation process, which in turn would make the proposed orientation program both timely and relevant. To switch commercials in mid-testimony, we can pay the parties and candidates now for transition planning, or pay the costs of delayed appointments, missed opportunities, and bad decisions later.

This subcommittee knows, of course, that the federal government already invests heavily in transitions. The General Services Administration already pays for most transition costs after the election is over, from moving vans for the incoming and outgoing president to staff and office space for the transition team. This subcommittee also knows that the federal government, or more precisely the federal taxpayer, also provides matching funds for the primary and general election campaigns, as well as $4 million to each party for the costs of hosting the national party conventions.

---

[9]Although I am obviously biased as both a former staffer at Pew and a new grantee, I believe that Pew continues to put its funding right where American democracy needs it most, whether in encouraging improvements in how the media cover politics through its projects on journalism, providing honest information on what Americans think about the issues of the day through the Pew Research Center on The People & The Press, or through its work on campaign reform and civic engagement. To paraphrase that old E.F. Hutton commercial, when Americans listen for the best ideas on how to renew democracy, they often hear Pew-funded projects talk.

If taxpayers are willing to see millions spent on balloons and confetti, one suspects they would gladly endorse a few hundred thousand dollars to do a little advance planning for the real event, the transition to governing.

The problem is that Congress and past presidents have seen pre-election transition planning by both candidates as wasted money. After all, one of the two is going to lose, meaning that at least one set of files will not be used. The candidates and their consultants are not much better. To be generous, some rightly worry that the public will read pre-election transition planning as a sign of over-confidence, while distracting the campaign team from the task at hand, winning the election. But there is also ample evidence that the political strategists would rather risk a failed transition than lose the inside track to a West Wing office.

One need only look back to 1992 to how that attitude plays out. Clinton's transition was an acknowledged disaster. Those celebrated combatants in the Clinton campaign war room spent exactly zero minutes thinking about what they would do after the election, short of keeping journals for future kiss-and-tell biographies. That attitude toward governing showed in the wild ride of missed appointments and bad decisions that marked the first year and beyond. By the time the Clinton team was up to speed, they had squandered what little political capital they had reaped from the president's razor thin victory.

The current crop of presidential hopefuls would be well advised to think further back in time to 1980 when Ronald Reagan broke all the political rules by establishing a transition operation in early spring. Not only was the operation completely separate from the campaign, thereby insulating it from the consultants, it was led by Reagan's most trusted advisor, Edwin Meese, and staffed by one of the country's top personnel experts, E. Pendleton James. The result was one of the fastest starts in modern presidential history, and dramatic budget and tax victories in a then-Democratic Congress.

Even with this head start, Reagan's cabinet entered office later than Carter's, which entered later than Nixon's, which entered later than Kennedy's. It was a harbinger of the complete breakdown of the presidential appointments process that plagues government today. Hence, Bush's cabinet entered later than Reagan's, and Clinton's entered later than Bush's. Those who survive the battering enter office frustrated and fatigued, in part because they so often endure the battering with little or no help from an under-staffed, over-taxed White House personnel office, and in part because the process itself has become a toxic mixture of uncertainty, insult, and delay.

Ultimately, it is up to the candidates to commit themselves to pre-election planning. The Democratic and Republican nominees could sweep away much of the old resistance by launching transition planning operations on the same day. But Congress can also improve the odds of that handshake by giving the national party committees a small allotment for pre-election planning. In doing so, Congress would send a strong signal that planning matters. As for wasted money, I strongly believe that the files from the losing campaign would find their way into the party archives for rescue four years later. Hope always springs eternal in the committees, after all.

Before concluding my testimony, let me note that there is good legislative precedent for providing pre-election planning funds. The Senate passed just such a proposal as part of the 1988 Presidential Transitions Effectiveness Act, which raised the transition allotments for both the incoming and outgoing administrations. Unfortunately, concerns in this body about spending money on what was sure to be at least one losing effort eventually led the Senate to withdraw the provision in conference.

It is important to note that the pre-election funding proposal had unanimous support in the other chamber and was based on bipartisan support from a veritable who's who of witnesses, including both chairman of the national party committees, former presidential transition directors, the Comptroller General, and representatives from the National Academy of Public Administration. The only objection to the proposal came from then-OMB Director James Miller who cautioned the committee to make clear that the funding would only go to major party candidates who have a legitimate chance to actually undertake a transition. With the needed refinements in hand, the committee approved the proposal on a 9-0 vote, with full Senate approval by voice vote in the spring of 1988.

It is also important to note that the committee considered several funding instruments for encouraging pre-election planning, including allowing the candidates to dedicate portions of their public financing toward pre-election planning. The committee concluded that a direct appropriation to the national party committees offered the greatest control over the actual expenditure of public funds for legitimate pre-election planning activities, and offered its strong endorsement of the General Service Administration as the logical place to administer these funds. As this subcommittee knows, GSA is responsible for administering presidential transitions funding after the election is over, and has ample experience judging appropriate expenditures.

I have no idea whether this idea could find the support needed for passage today. I must admit my own surprise at the ease with which the presidential pay increase passed, and congratulate this subcommittee for its courage in tackling what has long been considered a third-rail of legislative politics. But if we are to support an orientation program, as I believe we should, then I strongly suggest that this subcommittee has ample reason to increase the odds that the orientation program will come at the beginning, not toward the end, of the next administration. Providing a tiny subsidy to support pre-election transition planning is one way to do so.

Mr. HORN. I might add that the gentleman up there that you pointed to, when I went from the Hill down to the Brookings Institution as a senior fellow, I had a big dinner for a lot of leaders from the Hill and key staff people on bringing computers to Congress, which I had started in the Senate.

At the end of the dinner the individual to whom you referred said, "You're going to get that done over my dead body." So, when I came here, I introduced myself again to the chairman. He wasn't chairman of Government Operations at that time. And I said, Mr. Chairman, I am just curious. A mutual friend of yours and mine in Texas told me the story that when you first ran for office, you didn't like what your opponent was saying about you, it was a Democratic primary fight, and you put a .45 on the podium and said, if my opponent says in this debate what he said the last time, I am going to blow his brains out. And he paused on that and chomped on his cigar and said, "My opponent didn't have any brains," a colorful Member of the House.

Mr. Ornstein.

Mr. LIGHT. He was a great chairman.

Mr. ORNSTEIN. Mr. Chairman, it is a pleasure to be testifying with this group of four individuals. I had the wonderful honor of serving on the National Commission of Public Service with Elliot Richardson and working closely with him, as I did with Paul.

I did not have the privilege, I am thankful to say, of testifying in favor of the Presidential pay raise. I say it thankfully because I was out front the last time in 1988 and 1989, and I remember especially the only time I did Crossfire, I don't like to do a screaming shows, but I felt a public service commitment, and I got ganged up on by Pat Buchanan and Ralph Nader, which I continue to view today as a badge of great honor.

Mr. HORN. Saint Peter will pass you through.

Mr. OSE. Were you able to tell which one was which?

Mr. ORNSTEIN. I couldn't then, and I can't now, as a matter of fact. They merge into Ross Perot, I'm afraid.

I, of course, am very supportive of this piece of legislation, and I thank Dwight Ink for not only his decades of public service, but for continuing to champion some of these goals. Like Paul, I believe this is a small, essential step. We need to clarify the law in this regard, even though it could be done as the law is today. I also believe that the subcommittee should use this opportunity to broaden its focus into a number of other areas.

I very strongly endorse the notion of committing some money for preelection transition planning as a part of a broader effort, it seems to me, to move away from the notion that candidates have that it is presumptuous of them to even think of the notion of governing before the election. What happens is that after the election, they are exhausted. The winner is triumphant and needs some time to catch his breath. Everything that a new President-elect does is viewed by the press as wonderful, building them up before they tear them down, and there is no focus of preparing oneself or one's team generally. We drift through until the inauguration and then stumble along.

Steps that we can take now suggest that it is appropriate and necessary to think ahead so you can actually be prepared to govern, and that governing itself is something to be considered during the campaign by everybody.

At the same time it seems to me we have an ideal opportunity with an open Presidential contest, neither side seeing the strong need to tear down the other to keep things from working well afterwards, to really rethink or think through the whole gamut of issues surrounding the transition and the governing process. And I would like you look at the layering of political appointees, something that we dealt with very directly, that Elliot and I did in the Volcker Commission. The appropriate level of financial disclosure of political appointees. The desirability of reducing and standardizing the clearly confusing and overlapping forms that appointees must fill out, and rethinking the number and nature of nominees who require full FBI background checks.

The amount of time at every layer of this process and every level when you begin to think about making appointments is expanding. It is discouraging people from getting in, and it is keeping them from moving in when they take the jobs.

I would also like to see this as an opportunity to step back and see if we can take some small steps for a larger goal. I think of the broken window thesis of James Wilson that would send a signal that we want to change a culture that says if you come into public service, you are guilty until proven innocent, and begin to reestablish the notion that it is not such a bad thing to serve a period of time for your country.

As for the orientations themselves, for the last couple of decades I have been very active in a variety of the orientation programs that AEI and Brookings have done for new Members of Congress and that the Kennedy School does up at Harvard. Every Member who has been through those orientations knows when you come to Congress, it is a very different experience, whether you come from the business world or a legislative body. That is at least as true if not more so of top political appointees or lower-level political appointees, and it clearly is something that ought to be done and we ought to do now.

Let me just note, finally, Mr. Chairman, that I am heading up, along with Tom Mann at Brookings, and we are working very closely with Paul Light on a project that we call the Transition to Governing Project, and we are doing a variety of things to try to assist along this way. All of us want to work carefully with you.

One of the things that we are doing in conjunction with Martha Kumar, who is here today, is we are trying to prepare a piece of software that we hope will be the functional equivalent of turbo tax maybe crossed with the college applications software for appointees to make it easier to fill out those forms which now are a daunting task and probably discourage a number of people from serving at all. We really ought to rethink what goes into them in the first place.

[The prepared statement of Mr. Ornstein follows:]

Committee on Government Reform

Testimony of

Norman J. Ornstein

Resident Scholar
American Enterprise Institute

before the

House Subcommittee on Government Management, Information, and Technology
Committee on Government Reform

Oct. 13, 1999

on

"Presidential Transition Act Amendment of 1999"

10 a.m., Wednesday, Oct. 13, 1999
Room 2154, Rayburn House Office Building

Chairman Horn, I would like to start by thanking you and the other members of the House subcommittee on Government Management, Information and Technology for holding this hearing on the proposal to allow presidential transition funds to be spent on training and orientation for newly appointed officials. I strongly support the proposal on its merits. Newly appointed officials deserve the best training we can provide. But I also support this effort as an important first step in addressing a larger concern in our political culture, the need to foster an ethos of public service and to concentrate the minds of public servants and the citizenry at large on how we can best govern our nation.

I am pleased that you are holding the hearing now, before the presidential campaign reaches the formal stage of selecting nominees. Now is an especially appropriate time to focus on the transition ahead, and how we can improve the process of governing. I hope this hearing, on the relatively narrow but very important topic of orientation for appointees, will be followed by others that expand the focus to the transition to governing, including a look at ways we can broaden the pool of prospective nominees for significant federal office, remove unnecessary obstacles to their selection, nomination and confirmation, and encourage a climate more conducive to productive policy-making and implementation.

As for this bill, I support it for six reasons:

1. The proposal clarifies the purposes for which transition funds can be spent.
2. Presidential appointees are accomplished individuals, but most have little prior service in the executive branch.
3. Appointees see the need for training and orientation.
4. There are orientation sessions for Congress, Judges, and some executive branch personnel, and the response of participants has been good.
5. This proposal will remedy one aspect of a larger problem with presidential transitions and the appointments process.
6. The proposal sends a signal to the American people that effective governing is important.

1. Clarifying the purposes for which transition funds can be spent.

The Presidential Transition Act of 1963 authorizes that presidential transition funds shall be provided to the President-elect and Vice-President-Elect for "necessary services and facilities" "for use in connection with his preparations for the assumption of official duties as President or Vice President." Surely, the orientation of political appointees falls within this broad mandate. But making explicit the propriety of spending funds for appointee orientation is important for two reasons. First, the proposed language will reassure the transition team members that such spending is legal. Given the hectic transition period and the scrutiny of a new administration, transition team members may shy away from activities not specifically enumerated in the Presidential Transition Act. Second, the inclusion of such language will encourage transition teams to explore orientations for appointees. Indeed, I would favor strong language to underscore absolutely how desirable and important it is for any president-elect to provide such orientation.

2. Presidential appointees are accomplished individuals, but most have little prior service in the executive branch.

Presidential appointees hold important jobs and come to their positions with distinguished resumes. Heading an agency or a department is the public sector equivalent of being the CEO of a large corporation or the president of a university. While some appointees come from the public sector, most come from outside government, notably the private sector, non-profit world, and academia.

One of the strengths of our system of government is that it brings in talented people from outside of government to positions of public service. And political appointees often have impressive accomplishments, including managerial skills and experience. Nonetheless, appointees without executive branch experience may not appreciate features peculiar to government service such as Inspectors General, Congressional Oversight Committees, and Civil Service regulations. If we want to continue to entice the most accomplished people into public service, we should do everything possible to allow them to succeed. Months of bumpy on-the-job training is not the best way to do so.

3. Appointees see the need for training and orientation.

Sadly, appointees, when asked to look back at their service, express skepticism about whether they would serve again.[i] While there are a variety of reasons that appointees cite as to why they would not serve in government again, it is important to also consider appointees' recommendations on how to improve their time of service. One frequently mentioned recommendation is for better training.[ii]

It is not only the appointees who make this recommendation, but also those involved in their selection and appointment. Arnie Miller of the Clinton transition noted that he would "like to see much more cross-fertilization, using the interlude between nomination and confirmation for an orientation program."[iii]

4. There are orientation sessions for Congress, Judges, and some executive branch personnel, and the response of participants has been good.

For the past two decades or so, I have participated actively in orientation programs for new members of Congress, including the AEI/Brookings/Congressional Research Service program and the Kennedy School of Government orientation. These programs, along with others, such as the Heritage Foundation's and the parties' own orientations, have now served several generations of your colleagues, and have been widely lauded by them. Even though many new members of Congress have some elective experience, including legislative experience, nearly all recognize that Congress is different, with a number of unique characteristics, and that Congress considers a range of issues that will be new to nearly all new members. Whatever their ideology or party, lawmakers accept as a given that extensive orientation is a necessary experience for new members of Congress. They are not alone. New federal judges attend an orientation program put on by the Federal Judicial Conference. And since 1997, new executive appointees have participated in orientation sessions co-sponsored by the White House and the Council for Excellence in Government. The appointees who took part in the program have spoken highly of the program.[iv]

5. This proposal will remedy one aspect of a larger problem with presidential transitions and the appointments process.

This proposal is welcome because its aim is to help attract good people to government, give them the tools to succeed, and allow them to hit the ground running. But this proposal should be the beginning of a more comprehensive look at reforming the appointments process. I encourage you to support this proposal, but also to look at other measures that will expedite and smooth the selection, nomination and confirmation of political appointees. Subjects that your subcommittee might address are: the number and layers of political appointees; the appropriate level and detail of financial disclosure for appointees; the desirability of reducing and standardizing the confusing and overlapping forms that appointees must fill out; and rethinking the number and nature of nominees requiring full FBI background checks.

Along these lines, I would like to make you aware of a project I direct with Thomas Mann of the Brookings Institution. The Transition to Governing Project is an American Enterprise Institute Project in conjunction with the Brookings Institution and the Hoover Institution, funded by the Pew Charitable Trusts. Its aim is to assist all the branches of government in making a smooth transition to governing after the 2000 elections. We will be making recommendations as to how candidates can address issues of governance during the campaign, drawing lessons from past successful transitions, and seeking to remove obstacles that keep an administration from governing such as excessive paperwork for appointees and long delays for nomination and confirmation. Our project will work closely with Paul Light's Presidential Service Initiative Project to ensure that all of the phases of the process, the campaign, the transition, and the first days in office are directed at the goal of effective governance. Along these lines, we strongly support the notion that presidential candidates should engage in pre-election transition planning to begin the selection of potential appointees as early as possible. We believe that early identification of appointees, ample assistance to help them negotiate the nomination and confirmation process, and orientation will allow appointees to hit the ground running. One of the products of our project that new appointees might find especially useful is a computer software package to assist appointees in filling out the vast collection of forms required for nomination and confirmation. The software is being developed under a subgrant agreement with the University of Maryland Foundation and the work is being carried out by Martha Kumar of Towson State University and Terry Sullivan and Stephanie Haas of University of North Carolina.

6. The proposal sends a signal to the American people that effective governing is important.

Finally, I support this proposal because of the larger message it sends: governing is both important and possible. While our American system of government is still sound and the envy of the world, over the past thirty years one of our greatest strengths -- our commitment to effective governance and public service -- has begun to fade. The pre-eminent presidential scholar, Richard Neustadt, recounts how in 1960, the campaign staff of president-elect Kennedy was relieved that the successful campaign for office was over and that governing could begin. Winning an election was not merely a trophy to be savored, but an opportunity to govern in the public interest.

That sounds almost quaint now. Sadly, developments in our political culture have blurred the distinction between campaigning and governing, and now the end of effective governance is in danger of being forgotten. Pollsters and political consultants who were once employed primarily during election season, have now become permanent advisers to government officials. Almost every policy initiative is subjected to intensive polling and focus group research. Television advertisements from the political parties and interest groups fill the airwaves to support or oppose pending legislation. Private groups orchestrate legal challenges to laws they oppose, sue government and their adversaries, and use the discovery process to troll for politically embarrassing revelations about their opponents. The need for ever larger campaign war chests forces many elected officials to spend their time fundraising when they would prefer to focus on the problems facing our nation. Reporters cover campaigns as horse races, not in terms of competing visions or game plans for governing, and increasingly cover policy battles in Congress and the White House as campaigns, with the focus on who is winning and losing and not on the stakes for governance and public policy. In short, to use a term coined by another, we have moved into the era of the permanent campaign. All of these developments have contributed to an increasing cynicism about governing and public service.

It is of no use to wring one's hands about new developments in our political culture. They will not simply disappear from the political landscape. But if we cannot reverse the culture, we can find tangible ways of reshaping it. This proposal is one such way. It sends the non-partisan message that governing is important; that excellent people who leave important jobs in the private sector can come into government and make a contribution to the public good; and that the American people will support and encourage ways to make them more effective in their public service jobs.

There are many other worthy reforms that could be considered which would also contribute towards this larger end. The appointments process is too long, with positions often remaining vacant for many months or even years. There are too many layers of appointed and career officials. The heavier burdens of the nomination and confirmation obstacle course, combined with the culture of scandal that assumes everyone in public life is guilty until proven innocent, cause many to shy away altogether from public service. All of these problems will take time to solve or ameliorate. But we should not be so discouraged by the enormity of the problem that we fail to recognize the virtues of a small sensible reform such as the one before us today. Small but significant measures that support better governing are the way to begin to change attitudes that shape the larger culture.

---

[i] G. Calvin Mackenzie, " If You Want to Play, You've Got to Pay," in G. Calvin MacKenzie, ed., *The In- and Outers:Presidential Appointees and Transient Government in Washington* (Baltimore: Johns Hopkins University Press, 1987) pp.87-88.

[ii] John H. Trattner, *A Survivor's Guide For Government Executives: How To Succeed In Washington* (University Press of America, 1989).

[iii] *The 1997 Prune Book: Making the Right Appointments to Manage Washington's Toughest Jobs* (Madison Books, 1997). See also *Leadership in Jeopardy: The Fraying of the Presidential Appointments System* (Washington, D.C.: National Academy of Public Administration, November 1985).

[iv] Council for Excellence in Government, surveys of leadership conferences.

Mr. HORN. We thank you all. Given the situation on the floor and the voting schedule, I want to thank all of you as witnesses. If you don't mind, we would like to send you some questions that we might insert at this point in the record.

I should add to this that we have testimony not only from our witnesses today, but General Andrew J. Goodpaster, who I knew as Staff Secretary to President Eisenhower, the first time the White House had such a position, when he was a young major, and he will give us some documents, and then so will Pendleton James, Assistant to the President for Presidential Personnel during the Reagan administration, and he has submitted an item for the record. These are two very distinguished gentlemen who have a unique perspective on the Presidency and the transition process, and we welcome their process.

[The information referred to follows:]

THE
EISENHOWER
WORLD AFFAIRS INSTITUTE
AN AFFILIATE OF GETTYSBURG COLLEGE

October 7, 1999

The Honorable Stephen Horn
Chairman
Subcommittee on Government Management, Information and Technology
U.S. House of Representatives
Washington, DC 20515

Dear Mr. Chairman and Members of the Subcommittee:

I write to express my support for the Draft Bill to Amend the Presidential Transition Act of 1963 to provide for training of individuals a President-elect intends to nominate as department heads or appoint to key positions in the Executive Office of the President.

I served for six and one half years as White House Staff Secretary to President Eisenhower, and in senior military positions for nearly two additional decades.

The proposed amendment is in my view, on the basis of my experience, a constructive addition to the Transition Act. It should have positive value in terms of effective performance of governmental responsibilities beginning with the earliest days and weeks of the service of an incoming Administration. As part of the transition process, it can add significantly to the preparation of the officials who will serve in high policy and operational positions. Specifically, it could highlight functions of the Government, its methods and activities that take place in an environment often different in many respects from the previous business, professional or public experience of the individuals concerned. Even if limited in duration by virtue of the pressures of time, systematic orientation can be of signal importance and benefit on such matters as financial disclosures, avoidance of conflicts of interests, required record-keeping, personnel regulations and productive working relationships, to name but a few.

The procedure that this legislation will explicitly authorize will augment existing processes including the preparation of briefing books and activities of transition teams. It should be possible to focus on matters shown by experience to be most useful and valuable to the incoming high-level appointees. Key areas of major importance include congressional

1620 Eye Street, NW   Suite 703   Washington, DC 20006   (202)223-6710   Fax(202)452-1837

The Honorable Stephen Horn
October 7, 1999
Page two

relations (especially with key committees, subcommittees and staff), the functions of key offices of the Executive Office of the President, the duties and activities of past White House staffs, the ongoing work of the Career Services, as well as the role of outside interest groups and of the media. From the very outset, during the intense demands for actions and decisions to translate goals into policies and programs, a few hours of prior preparation of the kind this legislation authorizes seem certain to be of great assistance to the conduct of the government's business and the effective performance of its management functions.

For these reason, I strongly recommend passage of the proposed amendment.

Respectfully,

Andrew J. Goodpaster
General, U.S. Army (Ret)

Statement of Pendleton James
For the
House Committee on
Government Management, Information and Technology

Presidential Transition Orientations

Mr. Chairman and Members of the Committee:

I appreciate the opportunity to present this statement concerning the Presidential Transition bill, which I support with enthusiasm. Effective transitions are of critical importance in helping a new administration move forward with the agenda it placed before the American people during the election. Mistakes and unnecessary controversies during a transition or the first weeks after inauguration can haunt a new administration for some time. They detract significantly from the ability of a new president to address that agenda effectively or to develop the a good working relationship with congress.

My comments are based upon having been deeply immersed in the 1980-81 transition as Director of Personnel, as well as having served in the Reagan Administration as Assistant to the President for Presidential Personnel. Some transitions are better than others, but there is too much on-the-job learning compressed into a very short period.

The new team is faced with quickly translating campaign promises into policies and legislative initiatives while the team is still in the process of being put together. Everyone wants access to the incoming people the president-elect plans to appoint to top political positions before some of these men and women have a clear idea as to what their role will be or what the president expects of them. Much time is taken up with the exhaustive investigative and financial disclosure requirements that discourage a number of highly qualified people from completing the appointment process. The media has an insatiable appetite for prying for information about new programs that are still in an early brainstorming stage. Casual conversations by newcomers inexperienced in dealing with the press can easily spawn highly misleading and damaging stories about the new administration. The need to prepare for the first state of the union address and budget message soon after inauguration places unrealistic demands upon the president and his team as they strive to put the new government in place.

In this fast-moving environment of intense activity it is difficult to take the time to acquaint people with the complexity of the responsibilities they are about to assume. It is even more difficult to find the time to acquaint them with potential pitfalls they may encounter and to suggest ways in which to cope with the pressures that will escalate after inauguration. It is not surprising that able people with impressive backgrounds often have difficulty in making the sudden transformation from their prior professional life to governance at its most complex level.

Most transition briefings and briefing papers focus on program issues and options. This dimension of transition is clearly essential. But, apart from instructions about financial disclosures and violations of conflict of interest laws, most transitions provide little information about the types of operational missteps that often plague new political appointees, much less providing helpful suggestions about how to avoid them. Yet the most brilliant policies are of little use unless they can be implemented.

In other words, in the past we have tried to equip incoming key political appointees with information useful for developing the "what" of new program initiatives, but very little guidance on "how" to operate effectively in helping the president move his or her agenda forward. What is the role of White House staff, and how should they function? What is their relationship with departments and agencies? What are the most important approaches to effective executive-congressional relationships? How should one deal with the press? What is the nature of the complicated budget process? How does the public expect presidential appointees to behave, and how are the ethical expectations different than one encounters in business?

I believe the bill you are considering would substantially increase the likelihood that a president-elect would take steps to help his or her top political team avoid many of the pitfalls that so often embarrass and distract new administrations. It should help equip these new leaders with better techniques and approaches for coping with the difficult challenges of moving the government forward in the unique environment of Washington.

It seems to me that we should look carefully at our presidential transition arrangements for the purpose of determining what steps are needed to improve the effectiveness of our presidential transitions. I believe your bill is one of those steps that should be taken.

Mr. HORN. The hearing record will remain open for 2 weeks for additional insertions.

[The prepared statement of Hon. Jim Turner follows:]

STATEMENT OF THE HONORABLE JIM TURNER
GMIT LEGISLATIVE HEARING ON H.R.____, "THE PRESIDENTIAL TRANSITION PROPOSAL"
10/13/99

Thank you, Mr. Chairman. Our founding fathers designed the American government to be led by citizens who would step out of private life to provide a term of service to their country. Accordingly, each new Presidential Administration ushers in a new group of dedicated men and women committed to the highest ideals of public service. However, many of these talented new appointees have no experience when it comes to working in Washington.

Running the federal government is a complicated task, and I am sure that no one will disagree that the Washington environment is unlike any other. Therefore, it is important to ensure the seamless transition between the outgoing administration and the incoming administration. Before 1963, the primary source of funding for transition expenses was based on the party organization of the incoming President, and the efforts of volunteer staff. Congress, recognizing the need for a smooth transition, enacted the Presidential Transition Act of 1963 and amended the Act in 1976, to authorize federal funding and assistance for future incoming administrations. Congress authorized additional funds in 1988.

We are here today to assess the need for further changes to our transition process. The 1999 amendment to the Presidential Transition Act of 1963 would authorize the use of transition funds for the purpose of providing orientations for individuals the President-elect plans to nominate to top White House positions, including cabinet positions. It is expected that this orientation will provide a smoother transition for the new administration, thereby, eliminating mistakes and ensuring that our federal government will continue to function at a high level.

I appreciate the distinguished members who have taken their time to testify today and commend the chairman for his focus on this issue.

Mr. HORN. I want to thank the staff that prepared this hearing on both sides, Mr. George, the staff director and chief counsel for the subcommittee; Mr. Ebert on my left, policy advisor; Bonnie Heald, director of communications. She is in the back, seated back there; and Chip Ahlswede, our clerk; and P.J. Caceres, intern; and Deborah Oppenheim, intern.

And for minority we have Trey Henderson, counsel, and Jean Gosa, minority staff assistant; and we have our faithful court reporter Doreen Dotzler. Thank you very much.

With that, we will adjourn this session and go and vote.

[Whereupon, at 11:34 a.m., the subcommittee was adjourned.]

○

